Celebrating a Century *of primary science*

Edited by Max de Bóo and Audrey Randall

The Association for Science Education

Published by the Association for Science Education,
College Lane, Hatfield, Herts AL10 9AA
© The Association for Science Education, 2001

Executive editor: Helen Johnson
Design and page layout: Colin Barker
Printed by Black Bear Press Ltd, Cambridge, UK
ISBN 0 86357 328 2

Contents

Additional anecdotes, etc. scattered throughout by: *Max de Bóo,
Neville Evans, Sheila Jelly, Roy Richards* and *John Slade.*

Preface

The story of primary science is a fascinating and revealing one, which not only tells of innovative projects but of the role of particular people in the development of primary science and also of the impact of the changes on their own personal and private lives.

This book does not try to be an archive document about those projects; nor is it possible to include all the individuals to whom we are indebted, such as the late and much admired Len Ennever, the late Ros Driver and her influential work with the Children's Learning in Science (CLIS) Project, and the team and teachers involved in the SPACE research (Science Processes and Concept Exploration). What the editors have been able to do is make a collection of personal accounts and anecdotes which, when put together, give a 'family album' of historical details. As with any family album, people and projects overlap and 'new' ventures are seen to give birth to other developments.

At times the story might seem more like a patchwork than a single story, but the contributions all show the deep enthusiasm of the authors for children's education and for science. It is impossible to read these personal accounts without sensing the commitment, the amount of time spent working 'out of school hours' and the influence that these people and projects have had on education in the UK and further afield.

Some of the authors have been major influences, such as directors of projects, but the story also includes the fieldworkers who implemented and modified the excellent ideas which have inspired us all. Almost all of the authors have cut their teeth at the chalk face (if that is not mixing metaphors), and mostly in primary classrooms. There is inclusion of and reference to nursery education as well as secondary education.

Although the ASE was late in coming into the primary story (mid-century), the Association has now become a beacon for primary science in every way. We celebrate a century of primary science as well as the centenary of the ASE (Happy Birthday, ASE!).

The story of primary science, as told in this book, also tells of themes running throughout our professional lives:
• the status of the professional teacher, such as 'payment by results';
• the status of women in teaching;

- the state of school premises;
- the state of school resources in general and science resources in particular;
- the nature of elementary/primary education: the 3 'R's relative to a broader curriculum;
- the type of science in elementary/primary schools: nature study and/or 'science';
- the choice between practical, hands-on science or simply reading or being 'told' about it;
- the relative emphasis given to scientific enquiry skills and science content or knowledge;
- the particular scientific concepts chosen as suitable knowledge for young children to learn.

Many of these issues continue to give us problems today, in the twenty-first century. Perhaps that represents the eternal struggle between the profession and the funding agencies, especially when it comes to Government funding. We professionals have the outstanding priority of promoting children's access to good education, particularly science education, but this is always set in a context of 'time' – war-time, global events or movements, social concerns or economic pressures. We have to balance what we believe to be the 'best' education with what society can or wishes to afford, and we have to cope with changing attitudes towards teachers, ranging from teachers being seen as pillars of society (1930s–1940s) to being treated as political scapegoats (1990s).

Whichever time you are in when you read this book, or indeed however much time you have to read books (away from work or the classroom), we hope that you enjoy the story. We have been delighted and privileged to be characters in the story so far; many of you will be part of the untold story yet to come.

Max de Bóo and Audrey Randall
January 2001

1 Setting the scene

The evolution of primary science education, 1840–1950

Max de Bóo

In this first chapter a selection from the archives and material from Layton (1973) and Selleck (1972) has been chosen to show some of the changes that have taken place in primary education in general and science education in particular. Apart from an occasional comment here and there, I have let the archive material tell its own story. Wynne Harlen contributed archive material with her own commentary.

Elementary education in the nineteenth century

The middle of the nineteenth century was a time of great creativity, thinking, idealism and reform. In the 1840s, education was provided mostly by church-funded or other private schools; a few Board schools provided for the poor who could not afford to pay for education. The school-leaving age was 11–12 years but many poor families could not allow their children to attend school all the time: children were needed for paid work, in the fields, etc. The state schools reflected this low status. Elementary teachers at this time were usually untrained.

In his 'Address on National Education' Henry Chester, quoted in James Hole, *Light, more light*, London, 1860, pp. 14–15, stated:

... in 1839, so little attention had been given to the planning of schools, that they were commonly erected by the village bricklayer and carpenter by rule of thumb, without any plans at all. The organisation of schools had been little studied. A minimum education was given at a minimum cost. Babes of eight and ten years were set to teach other babes of the same age; ... Dr Bell's original plan of teaching poor children to

write by marking out letters with their fingers in shallow troughs of sand, had not long been abandoned. Of apparatus there was little but a few slates ... and a few writing desks fixed to the walls. The buildings were low, thin, dingy, ill-drained, often without means of warming, with cold, damp brick floors, often without proper conveniences; with no furniture but a teacher's desk, a few rickety forms, a rod, a cane and a fool's cap.

In the Census Report on Education, 1851, Horace Mann drew attention to the *'extraordinary educational advances achieved in the previous half century'.*

By the Education Report of 1860:

Government specifications for school buildings [are] well established and school books, apparatus and equipment have been improved immeasurably both in range and quality. [There are] recently established teacher training colleges. It [is] no longer necessary for schools to be staffed by untrained men and women, the former ... driven from the rougher struggles of life because of ill health or some physical defect.

The report reflected the incredible expansion of the numbers of both public and private schools in England and Wales:

Of the 15,000 or so elementary schools in existence in England and Wales by 1850, over a third had come into existence in the previous decade.

Introduction of science into the curriculum

New resources created opportunities for the achievement of new objectives and the mid-century was a period of considerable curriculum activity in elementary schools, one important aspect of which [was] the attempt to establish science as a basic ingredient of a general education.

The selection of scientific knowledge and skills for inclusion in the school curriculum inevitably involved drawing upon the repository of knowledge and skills accumulated in the science community. [There were also] prevailing views on the sort of intellectual activity involved in the pursuit of science. (Layton, 1973)

This set limits on the objectives of science studies in schools. The national preoccupation of English society at this time was applied or 'useful' science – such as the exter-

---

Not much change? Extracts from a school log book

August 15, 1864. *Adopted a plan of competition on spelling, called a boy out of the class and allowed the others from their reading lesson to select words likely to puzzle him; the boy who succeeded took his place. As a reward to the longest out I gave some marbles from a stock taken from late boys during the marble season who had remained playing instead of being in time at school. I am glad that after remaining in my desk for months they are likely to be turned into good account.*

September 4, 1865. *Attendance low today, several of the boys have been engaged to gather weeds by some neighbouring farmer.*

August 28, 1867. *Against my expectation the boy who was kept in yesterday returned today.*

Neville Evans

One hundred years ago 'science' was commonly taught through 'object lessons' such as that described in this extract from *The Infants' Mistress* of 4 May 1895

mination of insects destructive to timber in the dockyards. Furthermore, there was considerable conflict with the interests of the religious school bodies who dominated the educational scene. They did not wish to see science displace religious teaching. This was a time of enormous interest in astronomy (for navigation), geology, zoology and palaeontology. Darwin had just published his *Origin of species* in 1859. People felt that science might undermine religious beliefs.

Nevertheless,

decisions taken during the 1850s, and certainly before the introduction of the Revised Code in 1862, determined the bias of the elementary school curriculum for the remainder of the century and, indeed, so thoroughly infected the educational dispositions towards science as a school subject that traces are readily discernible today.

In the 1860s, one of the more notable developments was that of the Reverend Charles Mayo and his sister Elizabeth who wanted to *'quicken the powers of observation of their pupils and encourage skill in the arrangement and classification of objects'*. They pioneered a form of teaching which they regarded as preparatory to instruction in science. These two wrote and published a series of texts and lesson guides and sold *'cabinets of "Objects", such as minerals, natural and manufactured products, shells and familiar substances'*.

Skilled teachers had great success with this teaching approach: as one teacher said, *'No lessons produce more continued interest or more enlarge the minds of children than those Objects.'* Less skilled teachers, used to a more traditional transmission approach, simply taught their children to *'read about'* the Objects; they did not encourage observations and experiment. Yet another group of teachers converted the 'Objects' lessons into 'Object' lessons, where the chief focus was to bring out a religious or moral message from the materials in the collection.

In conclusion, although there was a growing demand for science in the elementary school curriculum, the nature of science studies was misunderstood. There was *'little recognition of science as a distinct mode of understanding'* – the development of reasoning. Indeed, for many years to come, *'the dependence on the written word for the transmission of science led to an ironic situation in which the use of observation and experiment to acquire knowledge was more read about than practised.'* (Layton, 1973)

3

The rise and fall of peripatetic science demonstrators

WYNNE HARLEN

With a view to the provision in the curriculum of their schools of some subject specially calculated to awaken and exercise the observing faculties of the children, the Liverpool School Board, acting on the advice of several eminent scientific gentlemen, in March 1877, resolved to introduce the systematic teaching of elementary science into their schools.

So began a statement by the clerk of the Liverpool School Board to the Royal Commission on Technical Instruction, 1884. Since the New Code (that governed 'payment by results') was in operation in 1877, he went on to explain that the subject fitted into the fourth schedule which allowed boys to be taught mechanics and girls 'domestic economy'. Whilst based on the syllabus for these subjects, the innovation was the introduction of experimental demonstration:

The method of teaching these subjects, which has been found by experience to be capable of producing very beneficial results to the scholars, is to combine ordinary lessons by the teachers of the school, with a system of experimental demonstrations given by means of appointed demonstrators. The apparatus required for the demonstrations is kept at a central laboratory, and is transferred from school to school as required, by means of a light hand cart. In this way each demonstrator is able to give from 18 to 20 demonstrations per week.

He then explained that the teachers, who were required to be present at the demonstrations, were expected to go over the subject of the demonstration between one and the next.

Evidence was produced in favour of the scheme from the improvement in examination results of the schools and from the examiner who marked the essays of candidates for scholarships. The examiner, a Cambridge Professor, was quoted as saying:

In two or three essays an amount of accurate scientific knowledge was manifested sufficiently considerable to attract my attention; on further inquiry, I found that the boys in question came from schools in which special scientific instruction has been given by the School Board. It seems not only to have been accurate and useful, but also to have laid hold of the boys' imagination and interested them.

Waterford School (1873–1932)

Reading through a book on the history of a local village, I noticed that the school had added Geography to the curriculum in 1893 and Science in 1899.

Audrey Randall

British Association report 1908

The following extract is from a report of the sub-committee on elementary experimental science, consisting of Prof. H. E. Armstrong, Mr Heller (secretary), Dr Kimmins, and Prof. Smithells, of the British Association Committee on Studies most suitable for Elementary Schools, published in *The School World*, September 1908:

... concerning 'the introduction into our elementary schools of a revised curriculum

based on practical studies ...'

Twenty years of progress

This branch of instruction in primary schools has been the subject of enquiry within recent years by two committees of the Association. The fundamental principles that should guide the teaching of elementary experimental science were clearly enunciated in the 1889 and 1890 reports... on the teaching of chemistry. ... The experience of the past fifteen years tends to emphasise rather than to modify the recommendations of those reports.

During this period, a remarkable transformation has taken place in the teaching of elementary science in this country, traceable in its origin to the 1889 and 1890 reports and to the indefatigable efforts of Prof. Armstrong and other members of that committee to achieve reform. In place of a large number of alternative specific subjects, none of them really fundamental in character, it is now insisted that there should be one general introductory course, indoctrinating that alphabet of scientific method and knowledge upon which the intelligent study of all specific sciences is based.

Early recognition of the importance of scientific enquiry skills

The reports directed attention to the overwhelming importance of [scientific] method in instruction by insisting that mental training and the formation of accurate habits of observation, of work, of reasoning, and of description were at the early stage of education of far greater moment than the accumulation of facts or the ability to answer examination questions on these facts. The deliberate intention to achieve these ideals must lie behind all teaching of elementary science.

To accomplish such ends it was found necessary to recommend a complete change in the methods of instruction commonly practised and in the attitude of the teacher towards his pupils and his subject. The method of experimental inquiry is the only natural method of gaining a knowledge of scientific facts; but such a method is the very antithesis of the didactic method of instruction too generally in vogue.

The practical method of inquiry now known as 'heuristic' has been defined as 'carefully directed inquiry'. Instruction should take the form of the experimental solution of a series of problems arranged in rational sequence. The motive for the experiment must be the outcome of skilful teaching, in which the teacher has led his pupils from the known to the unknown and to a clear conception of the problem to be solved; the experiment should not be merely an occasional effort to substantiate one of the many facts that the teacher has told his class.

Teaching in which experimental results are to form the basis of reasoning and the basis for new problems should involve precision; the facts should at least be true, or the method is obviously of no more purpose than those it is intended to supplant. Measurement must be the basis of experiments and quantitative analysis should be encouraged.

Influence of the British Association reports on schools

The reports referred to have profoundly influenced directly and indirectly the science teaching in secondary schools ... In the primary schools great changes have also taken place; the higher grade schools of the larger urban education authorities are usually well equipped, and a teacher of experimental science is appointed to take charge of the laboratories. Increased provision has also been made ... in training colleges for the teaching of experimental methods.

In many urban centres, from reasons of economy and because few of the ordinary teachers possessed an acquaintance with apparatus and experimental method, special staff of peripatetic science demonstrators were appointed: these usually taught periodically in the schools in their district, usually carrying their apparatus about with them. The scheme of instruction followed was knowledge of 'Mechanics' but embraced a superficial treatment also of hydrostatics, the laws of force and motion, heat, chemistry and electricity. In some cases, the individual ability of the demonstrator made the lessons useful and interesting but the system was only adopted as a matter of expedience and the scheme of instruction has been far too disjointed to lead young children to much real knowledge that could be applied in later life. Under this system of peripatetic instructors, little effort has been made as could be made to co-ordinate instruction in science with that in other subjects, such as composition, arithmetic, reading and drawing. Between the visits of the special instructors, the class teacher was supposed to revise the lesson with the assistance of the apparatus that the instructor had left with him; this revision was done in a half-hearted way, and led to undesirable methods of memorising digested information.

A CALL FOR SCIENCE SUBJECT SPECIALIST TEACHERS IN SCHOOLS AND 'TRAINING' FOR NON-SPECIALIST CLASS TEACHERS

It appears to be undesirable that the system of peripatetic instructors should continue, except as a temporary expedient and until each school possesses permanent and sufficiently qualified teachers of experimental science. The services of a staff of specialists should be employed in instructing the ordinary teachers, most especially in the methods of teaching and organising of science studies. The rigid adherence to the class-teacher system used in most primary schools should be abandoned, and the best qualified teacher should be responsible for the science in several classes, if not for the whole school, and it should be the business of the head teacher to arrange adequate co-ordination of instruction for teachers in that position, and linking arithmetic with science.

So, after 15 years of demonstrations from the 'handcart' science specialists, the British Association recommended that the system of peripatetic science teachers, which had clearly spread beyond Liverpool, should not continue. The reasons given showed how much priorities were changing. First, the science demonstrations were not connected to other subjects studied by the children. Second, the content was criticised for being superficial and not leading to 'real knowledge' that could be useful in later life. Third, the schools' teachers were not doing a good job between demonstrations and were using 'undesirable methods' which involved children in rote-learning of poorly digested information. Instead, the sub-committee recommended that schools should appoint a well-qualified teacher to advise other teachers and to teach the science in several classes and that it should be the head teacher's responsibility to ensure that there was co-ordination of science with other subjects.

As ever, one generation's innovation is another's cause for concern.

Elementary/primary education, 1914–1939

The experiences of the First World War left a lasting impression on many people involved in young children's education. Many teachers had gone to war and never returned; others had returned too traumatised ever to teach again; food shortages and other deprivation had led to widespread absence from school and the 'flu epidemic of 1918–1919 killed many children as well as adults.

One positive outcome emerged from this bleak period. Statistics gathered by the Ministry of War revealed a nation racked by poverty: many of the men who enlisted from the working classes were unfit to fight. A childhood spent with a wholly inadequate diet, poor living conditions and an early start to a working life was not the best preparation for fit, healthy fighting men. And although everyone said of the war, 'It was the war to end all wars', the Government did not want to be in the position of relying upon a nation of unfit, unhealthy young men.

The answer was an attempt to make some provision for the poor, partly by improving conditions for children in the state elementary schools (better buildings, free

A typical primary school class in the early twentieth century contentrating on the three 'R's (photo courtesy of Little Ealing Primary School)

7

school milk and free school meals in cases of real deprivation). Some of the changes of these times were temporary, others were more permanent. In 1914, the Education (Provision of Meals) Act was passed. The Fisher Act of 1918 expanded the remit of the local education authorities and raised teachers' salaries, funded school medical inspections, etc.

Alas, the 'good times' were short-lived. Three years later, in 1921, the Geddes Committee on National Expenditure was recommending massive financial cuts in public spending on schools. The Geddes Committee wanted to raise the school admission age to 6 years, reduce free places, increase class sizes, cut school meals, end medical inspections and lower teachers' salaries. Teachers were forced to accept a 5% cut in salaries (1922) and, in spite of protests and strikes, further cuts in 1924 (1%) and 1931 (10%). By then, teachers' morale was described as the lowest of all time. [If we compare this with teachers' morale today, at the end of the twentieth century, it does appear that whenever Government has problems (expenditure or the need for scapegoats), the teaching profession is one of the first to be sacrificed.]

The progressive movement in education

The First World War had deeply affected others with a concern for children and/or education. Educational progressives had begun to argue the case for the child being of central importance in education. Maria Montessori's book, *The Montessori method*, had been translated into English in 1912 and by 1914, 'New Education' was challenging all elementary school teaching as having too much stern discipline and too narrow a curriculum.

Elsewhere, John Dewey was arguing for improved scientific education:

One of the only two articles that remain in my creed of life is that the future of our civilization depends on the widening spread and deepening hold of the scientific habit of mind; and that the problem of problems in our education is therefore to discover how to mature and make effective this scientific habit. (Dewey, 1910)

The progressive movement really began to take off after the war. In spite of financial cuts, changes in attitudes were influencing national practice. The Hadow Report of 1926 stated that *'elementary education is associated with impoverishment and class distinction'* and should in future be called *'primary education'* as *'the first stage in an educational process that [leads] all children to secondary education at the age of 11 years'*. The report went on to say that the primary school would best serve the children's future by:

... a single minded devotion to their needs in the present and the question which most concerns is not what children should be – a point on which unanimity has hardly yet been reached – but what, in actual fact, children are. ... the central consideration by which the curricula and methods of the primary school must be determined, is the sum of the needs and possibilities of the children attending it.

The report goes on to question the existing practice of didactic teaching, with a body of knowledge to be imparted and learnt by rote, and argues the case for developing children's skills and attitudes to learning:

primary education would gain greatly in realism and power of inspiration if an attempt were made more generally to think of the curriculum less in terms of depart-

ments of knowledge to be taught, and more in terms of activities to be fostered and interests to be broadened.

Education must be regarded, not as a routine designed to facilitate the assimilation of dead matter, but as a group of activities by which powers are exercised, and curiosity aroused, satisfied and again aroused.

This was the period when Piaget was carrying out his studies of children (publishing in 1926, 1929, etc.), and although his research had not originally been intended for educational purposes, he succeeded in influencing education for the rest of the century. Other innovative thinkers at that time (Montessori, Susan Isaacs, Dewey, Froebel, Pestalozzi, Margaret Macmillan and Gesell) were consulted by the Hadow Committee in preparing their 1933 report, *Infant and nursery schools*. The report clearly espoused principles of the importance of physical, mental and emotional development in young children.

Selection at 11+

As a result of Hadow (1926), 1931 saw the establishment of secondary 'modern' schools that were supposed to eliminate the stigma of non-academic pupils by putting the emphasis on a 'practically-based' education. However, sorting out the 'sheep from the goats' or selecting children for secondary modern or grammar schools put great pressure on primary schools. The achievements of children at the age of 11 would determine which type of secondary school they would attend. [In the year 2000, primary schools were again under pressure, with key stage 2 SATs, school league tables, etc.]

The full impact of the 11+ examination came after the Second World War, but in the 1920s and 1930s the pressure on the primary schools increased, particularly the pressure to obtain the maximum number of scholarships which opened the door to a prestigious grammar school education to primary school children. As the Secretary for Elementary Education, Lancashire Education Committee, stated:

There is no doubt that the shadow of the examination (which is important only for the minority) still darkens the way of too many children through the last year or so of the primary course. As far as school attainments are concerned, the examinations are commonly limited to the subjects of Arithmetic and English, and naturally enough the schools are apt to be driven to deal with these two subjects in their 'testable' aspects. (Perkins, 1936: 279)

J. Compton (West Riding Administrator) added:

It would be hard to find the head teacher of a junior school who does not believe that the effect of the examination held in the last year is cramping and depressing! (Compton, 1937: 365)

Nature study and science

In the nineteenth century, nature study had been emphasised, partly as a result of the ideals of the 'Romanticists'.

There was a misunderstanding about nature study in schools. The 'naturalist' is interested in observing nature, more or less at random, chiefly for personal enjoyment. This is very different from a 'scientist', who works with a systematic body of knowledge, and whose chief aim is to extend that knowledge further. As Dewey said (1938: 6–7), *'there is always a danger in a new movement that in rejecting the aim and methods of that which it would supplant, it may develop its principles negatively rather than positively and constructively.'*

There was a further conflict between 'nature' and 'books' as if these were exclusive methods of learning. The nature table became associated not just with observation but with identification, which became an end in itself. Some teachers simply taught the names of trees as a substitute for observation of real trees. Attempts to make the unfamiliar familiar resulted in: (a) nature stories that anthropomorphised natural objects, such as *'The discontented pine tree'* which didn't like its leaves; (b) baby talk that took analogies to extremes, such as *'The mummy bird and the daddy bird...'*, *'The baby seed in its cradle.'*

Nevertheless, there was a move to introduce children to physical science, as reported in a pamphlet written for the Science Masters' Association (later ASE) by Savage (1932), 'The teaching of "colour" in elementary courses of science':

The general movement in the teaching of science is towards an appreciation of physical phenomena ... The essential facts [need to be] fully and convincingly demonstrated by the teacher or by the pupil for himself.

Science masters [all agree] that so far as possible, everyday phenomena and common experiences should be utilised as the foundation stones of school work in science. In this respect, Colour has scarcely a rival. For once in a while, town and country stand almost on equal terms. The pageant of Nature provides for the country the whole year round in field and wood and sky, whilst if fog and smoke, bricks and mortar deny these to the town child, there is compensation in the posters on the hoardings, the gay colours of the shop windows, and at night, the colours of the electric light signs. Even the fog and smoke assist, as one may see by comparing the colours of the near and distant sides of a long street. (pp. 3–4)

[Note that fogs and smogs in London and northern industrial towns were taken for granted at that time! The Clean Air Act had not yet been introduced.]

Moving away from narrow attitudes and reductionist policies

The nation's schools, a report from the Ministry of Education, England & Wales (HMSO, 1931), stated clearly that:

The aim of the junior school will be to make the fullest use of the lively interest of children at this stage in their own personal achievements and their active curiosity about the world around them ... the curriculum must be thought of in terms of activity and experience rather than knowledge to be acquired and facts to be stored. This will entail a departure from the traditional methods of class instruction in favour of individual work in acquiring skills and in project activities pursued in groups.

Further weight was given to effective policies and practices in primary education by the Education Act of 1944.

Many teachers and schools took these ideas up with enthusiasm, none more so than the teachers in Greater London. A few years after the Ministry report, Graham Savage, Education Officer for London County Council (LCC), published a report, *Trends in primary education* (Savage, 1950). He based his report on documents written by the Chief HMI of the time. Both men wanted to applaud the best practice and support innovative primary education that put the child's learning as the central focus, rather than the rigid formality of teaching the 3 'R's. [It is always interesting to compare the attitudes and policies of such influential people; for example, fifty years from now, what will recent Secretaries of State for Education or Chief HMIs be remembered for?]

The preface of Dr Savage's report states that *'This pamphlet [is] based on a report by the Chief Inspector (Dr A. G. Hughes)'*:

During the education year of 1947–8, thirty one inspection reports were written on London primary schools attended by infant and junior children. The pamphlet summarises the overall impression of the work going on in schools, including a great deal of pioneer work.

The most striking impression is that primary education is on the move. The rate is by no means uniform in all the schools inspected: in a few it is rapid and adventurous;

The trials of a visiting inspector

Know your place (1)

On arrival at the school, the inspector saw that the headteacher was giving a pupil a good telling-off.

Even so, the inspector cut across and announced, *'I am ... ..., the inspector you are expecting.'*

'Fine,' said the head, *'excuse me a moment, but take a seat.'*

The inspector unwisely persisted and introduced himself a second time. To his everlasting glory, the head replied, *'I heard you. I am busy. Take two seats if you wish.'*

Know your place (2)

The inspector was visiting a class of infants. Spotting an empty chair at one of the tables, he sat down and wrote a few words in his notebook. This was observed by the pupils sitting at the same table. The conversation was opened by one of them:

'Who are you?'

'I'm the inspector.'

'What did you do in your book?'

'I wrote some words.'

'Can you do joined-up writing?'

'Yes.'

'Do you start your sentences with a capital letter?'

'Yes.'

'Well, you're sitting at the wrong table.'

Neville Evans

in some it is slow and cautious; in others it is as yet hardly discernible. But in all schools, the emphasis is changing – away from a situation in which classes are being taught most of the day sitting still or standing rigidly in lines, towards one in which individual children are actively learning through experiences that appeal to their natural interests.

The change is profoundly affecting the whole life of primary schools, from the quality of their social atmosphere to the character of their oral lessons. Oral teaching is … gradually changing from a rather artificial talk punctuated by questions and answers to something more nearly resembling natural, animated conversation. In oral lessons, whether given to individuals, groups or classes, children have opportunities for taking the initiative, and of being active participants and not merely passive recipients.

Infants schools were the first to break away from formal class teaching … [and the active approach] is now spreading to junior schools, slowly in the face of difficult conditions and against the inertia of a tradition imposed by conditions even more difficult than those of today. More important and significant, the movement in both infants and junior schools is expanding beyond the learning of the 3 'R's …. Teachers are now devising methods designed to educate children through creative activities, … for example, fact-giving lessons in separate subjects, history, geography and nature study, are to some extent being replaced by projects in which children take the initiative and acquire knowledge, not only from books but also by exploring the school and its neighbourhood, and where facilities exist, by experimental work and observation in gardens and science rooms.

For example, a class of 42 boys and girls aged 8 to 9 years, took as a project 'My House'. Very soon the class divided into 6 groups, each pursuing a special topic suggested by the main centre of interest. A group of 7 boys studied the water system. They began by following the water pipes in their school; they drew lively, intricate sketches of their discoveries, accompanied by notes in simple, direct, terse English; they appealed to their teacher for information, some of which was incorporated into their notes.

The interest spread in many directions: to sewage pipes, gas pipes, the oldest pipes in the world and submarines. The work did not stop short at exploring the school in school hours; the boys went on to explore the pipes in their own houses, and the following note accompanying a sketch of a house in section indicates the absorbing interest aroused: 'This is a house with the walls cut off. There are 16 numbers and 16 arrows which show the pipes and cisterns and taps.' 'Do you ever wonder', wrote one boy, 'where the things you throw down the pan go to? It goes under the house to the sewers. There it dashes over the sloshy mud. Men work there and pick out anything of value. They also have sharp knives to kill rats, they are about the size of a cat.'

The new approach to primary education has the great merit that it stimulates interest and gives scope for all pupils, irrespective of the degree or kind of their ability; it is valuable for the most gifted as well as the most backward pupil.

Lack of facilities and resources for science

Savage (1950) goes on to state that many of the capital's junior schools were still having problems in 1947–48, resettling themselves and their pupils after evacuation, suffering from lack of resources and partial or whole-scale destruction of school

12

buildings during the war. Class sizes at this time were 40.

Nevertheless, the Chief HMI and Savage (1950) agreed that:

more emphasis should be placed on learning by pupils and less on teaching by teachers, that what children do and learn in school should be related to what they do and learn out of school, that there ought to be more activity, less abstract arithmetic, a greater touch of reality, less class instruction, more creative expression.

There are poor classrooms, few facilities – lack of space in the classroom, lack of space for a science corner, for aquaria, for keeping plants and animals, for a nature table ... for craftwork benches and a sink. ... Children are working in corridors, cloakrooms, in the head-teacher's room and on staircases.

There is an atmosphere of gloom created by poor gas lighting, by the dingy appearance of school decorations. ... Athough teachers make colourful displays to relieve the gloom, we need local programmes of redecoration and electrification.

Drastic reforms are needed inside and outside the school ... children should see trees and flowers and grass [many schools were surrounded by bomb sites at this time]. A few twigs in a jam-jar on the classroom windowsill are a poor substitute for growing trees ... Every school should have at least a small garden. (p. 8)

Constraints imposed by the common entrance test and the 3 'R's

Another handicap ... is the anxiety about the results of the common entrance test (11+)... The emancipation of junior schools from external attainment tests may not be possible at present but it is an ideal we should not abandon. It is probably more important to foster thought and research to this end than to strive to refine still further, our methods of testing children in English and arithmetic.

Schools and classes who adopt the new approaches reflect not only happy, active, orderly behaviour but an enthusiastic attitude to work. Basic facts, essential skills and a wide general knowledge are acquired and retained. In the best schools, fresh interests and new activities are constantly emerging, often from the children themselves, and it is reasonable to hope that such self-chosen experiences may have a permanent influence on children's attitude to learning.

These new approaches were adopted by some schools because they were dissatisfied with the results obtained by formal drill methods in reading, spelling, composition, handwriting and arithmetic. In the past, in our anxiety to teach the 3 'R's formally ... we have ... subjected many young children to unnecessary drudgery...

... in many schools [focused] training in the 3 'R's now falls into its proper place – not as a preliminary task in preparation for more interesting experiences but rather a secondary task arising from such experiences ... coming towards the end of the school day ... and as such, the children enjoy them no less than they enjoy the activities that call for more physical movement.

Some junior teachers and parents and interested members of the public think of this approach as 'sentimental pandering to children's whims' – from a misunderstanding and insufficient knowledge of the aims and methods of modern primary schools. Primary teachers need every possible encouragement ... more space, better equipment ... and above all, smaller classes.

The full results of helping children to become [enthusiastic, independent learners] cannot be measured by an examination at the age of 10; primary education is an act of faith and its results, together with those of secondary education, must be looked for in years ahead in the excellence and fullness of adult life. (p. 10)

For all who would assess others (teachers? Ofsted inspectors? Chief HMIs?)

A man was employed as a wheeltapper by a railway company. His job was to walk along the length of a train of carriages tapping each wheel with his hammer. He could tell from the characteristic sound from each wheel whether the wheel was fit for service.

One day, after completing his inspection, he reported to the depot manager that every wheel was defective. Greatly surprised, but mindful of his duty, the manager followed the advice and replaced every wheel.

Once again, the wheeltapper repeated his scrutiny and, once again, reported the same outcome. Once again, the manager, despite severe misgivings, replaced every wheel.

For the third time, the wheeltapper walked, tapped, listened and reported. As before, his instruction was 'Change every wheel.'

But this time, the manager said, 'Can I check your hammer, please?'

Neville Evans

From *Humour, muse, enterprise* (1998) published by The Leonard Cheshire Homes and Ty Hafan, The Children's Hospice in Wales.

Comparable changes in Scotland at this time

A highly influential document from the Scottish Education Department in 1946, *Primary education* (HMSO, Edinburgh) compared current education with information from the 1872 Education (Scotland) Act. This Act had stated that:

The Primary curriculum is rigid and uninformed. 'Payment by results' is an unsatisfactory form of assessing the income of a school board – and often the headmaster. (p. 3)

'Payment by results' depended on the number of pupils who succeeded, as a result of the annual 'inspection', in passing from one standard to another: *'This had serious and far-reaching results which affect many of our schools to this day.'* Teachers could also lose their jobs! The 1946 document argued that whilst good schools with clever pupils obtained good results, the less gifted pupils *'existed in a chilly atmosphere of disapproval and intellectual bewilderment'*.

Some of the criticisms of formal primary education (1946)

The hard division between 'subjects' is a logical and adult conception that is justified neither by life experience nor as a natural way of learning. ... The whole atmosphere is too 'academic', verbal rather than real, cut off from the living interests of childhood ... [Whole] class teaching is seriously questioned, on the ground that it bores equally those who know the lesson already and those who will never know it, and that it rests on the baseless assumption that all or most can be brought up to a certain 'standard of attainment' in a given time. (p. 20)

Children learn differently from adults ... each child must find as well as make his own world. The ordinary experiences of children are generally more vivid than those of adults; the size and domination of things present and things around are much greater; time moves more slowly ... they accept as permanent what we know to be transitory. ... Because of this, children ... should not be troubled with facts and ideas outside their natural range of interests and receptivity ... not given a body of knowledge to be learned [by rote]. (p.44)

Emphasis on experiential learning

There is no valid reason why nature knowledge should not include the works of man, as in fact it nearly always does. One can as well begin from the city streets and shops and arrive at the farms and fields and hedgerows, as proceed in the opposite direction; provided that at some stage opportunity is given for all children to learn something about the country and the life of the town – and also, we may add, of the seashore and the sea and the skies above.

In these studies, the role of the child is that of adventurer, collector and questioner; that of the teacher to inspire, explain and encourage. The materials of the lessons should, whenever possible, be the real objects. It is very much easier and much more real to have a talk about a cow or a potato or the North Star in the presence of these familiar objects. The cow must, however, be seen outside of school, and the North Star out of school hours. ... Teachers who loathe the introduction of creepy-crawly things into the classroom should try to overcome their aversion because of the enthusiasm of the pupils and the sense of reality given to the subject.

Recommended content

CURRICULUM STUDIES SHOULD INCLUDE:
Growth in plants and animals
Habitats
Reproduction
Food chains and ecosystems
Man and nature links
Beauty, intricacy and wonder of nature
Environmental sensitivity
Earth and beyond
Weather
Water cycle

[Compare this list with today's National Curriculum for England: many of the above are found in the Science 2000 curriculum, but not 'Beauty, intricacy and wonder'.]

The Scottish attitude towards research in education (1946)

If all educational problems had been completely solved and children completely standardised, experiment would be a waste of time and research an antiquarian hobby. But as social needs and ideas change, education must also go on changing and developing. Experiment and research, by which alone such development may be brought about in a fruitful and comprehensive way, must continue to be a vital element in any system of education.

The ways by which children learn cannot be reduced to a set of rules of universal application. They depend much on time, place, circumstance; and most of all on personal disposition and relationships. So the good teacher will always be 'trying something new' and such an attitude will always appeal to ... children. ... There are other experiments that cannot satisfactorily be carried out by a single teacher or a single school without corroboration from elsewhere or without a wider field of enquiry. From this arises the need for scientific research on a wide basis, national or even international. Every teacher should feel that he or she is a participant in research; whether engaging in it or benefiting from it – preferably both. [The Scottish Council for Research in Education already existed in 1946 and was very active.]

Members of education committees, and indeed some teachers, complain about the lack of intelligibility of some research reports. The fact is that any conclusions or results of educational research must be couched in language that is specific and cautious and generalisations must be accurate. This does inevitably lead to a jargon which is less comprehensible. However, the results of these researches should be presented and published in a summarised accessible form to allow easier access to the non-academic. Speculation must be free and investigation disinterested. Results obtained may be negative, there may emerge nothing of any practical value, or a practical result may come almost incidentally as a by-product. There is not a new germ under every microscope or an Eldorado at the end of every voyage. Nevertheless, there must be public educational funds [to research] new facts, ideas and techniques that will sooner or later, and in some form or other, be of educational benefit in schools. (p. 112)

While in the scientific sense, the majority of teachers may not be researchers, all must be experimenters, trying out new ideas ... as a good teacher never ceases to experiment to the end of her teaching days. (p. 114)

This seems to be a fitting note on which to end the chapter that leads into the wonderful experimentation and research into primary science education that began to take place in the 1950s and onwards. These had a formative influence on us – both teachers and children. Many of the giants on whose shoulders we now stand are alive today. In the following chapters, you will read some of their recollections of the way primary science has evolved in the second half of the twentieth century, together with some of the people who implemented their ideas.

References

Compton, J. (1937) The junior school, from the point of view of an administrator. In *The year book of education.* West Riding of Yorkshire.

Dewey, John (1910) Science as subject-matter and as method. In *Science*, **31**, 27.

Dewey, John (1938) *Experience and education.* New York: Macmillan.

Hadow/Board of Education (1926) *Report of the Consultative Committee on The Education of the Adolescent.* London.

Hadow/Board of Education (1931) *Report of the Consultative Committee on the Primary School.* London.

Hadow/Board of Education (1933) *Report of the Consultative Committee on Infant and Nursery Schools.* London.

Layton, David (1973) *Science for the people.* London: Allen & Unwin.

Ministry of Education (England & Wales) (1931) *The nation's schools.* London: HMSO.

Perkins, W. H. (1936) *Educational year book.* Lancashire Education Committee.

Savage, E. G. (1932) The teaching of 'colour' in elementary courses of science. In *Modern Science Memoirs*, 13. The Science Masters' Association. London: John Murray.

Savage, E. G. (1950) *Trends in primary education.* The County Hall, London County Council.

Scottish Education Department (1946) *Primary education – a report of the Advisory Council on Education in Scotland.* Edinburgh: HMSO.

Selleck, R. J. W. (1972) *English primary education and the progressives, 1914–1939.* London: Routledge and Kegan Paul.

2 The progressive movement and its effects ∽

Gwen Allen

From Froebel to shared ownership: moving towards a child-centred approach

Gwen Allen started teaching in 1936 and taught biology/science for 16 years before becoming a lecturer in FE and HE colleges. She worked in the Froebel Educational Institute (now Froebel College, University of Surrey) during which time she was the Head of the Natural Science Department. Together with Joan Denslow (a junior school teacher) she wrote the 'Clue Books for Natural History' (Oxford University Press) which are still used in many primary schools today.

My developing ideas about science education

As a young teacher in 1936, I set out with the idea that one planned a limited theme of knowledge to *convey* to pupils to be *learned* by them. However, my father was Head of a 'Craft School' where a practical approach was much appreciated by children of coalminers and tinplate workers as well as by their parents. Very aware of this approach, I was intrigued by the excited responses to free investigations during lunch hours of grammar school girls and lively discussions with secondary modern girls (1940s) on topics familiar to them. Over the years my approach to learning evolved.

In 1955, I joined the Natural History Department of the Froebel Educational Institute. I began to appreciate the work of people who had a very real concern for children and their education. Children had often been treated without respect and frequently considered just as child labour. I began to recognise what a great deal of thought and practice had been invested to improve children's conditions and education.

The great innovators in childhood education

Early in the 1830s, Froebel had begun lecturing to spread and justify his ideas. Teaching was then viewed as the strictly regulated 'acquisition of facts', irrespective of the children's readiness to understand and assimilate them. Froebel found, as we still do today, that it was a continual battle to try to change this fixed pattern of teaching to a system of free development of ideas.

Over the next 100 years, education and its methods, aided by many dedicated men and women, grew and developed. For example, Dr Maria Montessori was concerned with developing the senses of nursery children, agreeing with Froebel's ideas but not his methods. Margaret Macmillan supported the need for medical examinations in schools.

In 1933, Susan Isaacs's work in the Department of Child Development was influenced by research in the USA that linked child development with the whole school curriculum. Nathan Isaacs, later a Governor of the Froebel Foundation, was determined that this country needed to do likewise. To achieve this, he and many others gave lectures and talks to universities, colleges and educational establishments. In 1944, the Education Act began to embody many of the demands arising from this.

Infants in the 1950s gaining some hands-on experience with sand and water play (photo courtesy of Little Ealing Primary School)

The pace of change accelerates

In 1958 the National Froebel Foundation published a lecture by Nathan Isaacs entitled *Early scientific trends in children*. In 1959, The Association of Teachers in Colleges and Departments of Education published *Science in the primary school*.

At about this time, Miss Barbara Rapaport, responsible for junior education in the Froebel Institute, asked me to work with her Children's Club to provide exploration into the broadly scientific field. I thus became involved in the fascinating enquiries inspired by Nathan Isaacs to test the value of introducing pre-scientific activities in primary schools.

In 1961, the Ministry of Education produced a very instructive pamphlet, *Science in primary schools, No. 42*, drawing attention to the increasing part science played in our lives and the need for its appropriate inclusion for children of all ages. In that same year, a lecture given to the British Association for the Advancement of Science, 'Approaches to science in the primary school', resulted in a limited enquiry, acting through the National Froebel Foundation, in which a number of teachers volunteered to keep records of interests developed in their own classrooms. They agreed to send reports each term for a panel, led by Nathan Isaacs, to assess.

As a result of this, in 1966, the National Froebel Foundation published booklets (e.g. *Children learning through scientific interests*) and co-operative study schemes for teachers, quoting examples from 5–10 year-old children with some detailed accounts of their development. It aimed to persuade teachers of the need for adaptability to a new and vital way of learning which involved the children sharing responsibility for its content – a revolutionary idea! 'Finding-out activities' emphasised the need to expand the books and equipment available to meet the increasing demands for wider, more exciting and better-understood studies. The message was that when children have some ownership of the focus of their studies, their attitude to the subject improves and they become independent learners.

Teachers' feedback was helpful, critical and constructive. In general, they concluded that awareness of age as well as academic abilities is important for fruitful starting points and for appreciating children's assumptions, while practical activities are a vital accompaniment to understanding throughout the age range. The observation of characteristics such as colour, shape and texture was appreciated as a delightful and exciting part of the whole field of learning.

Developing scientific attitudes

Some teachers queried the apparent absence in the scheme of human and social problems but others recognised their beginnings in the nursery, with its 'Wendy House' and 'Shop' among other activities involving more basic scientific experiences. All of these activities could lead to simple scientific attitudes being naturally assimilated as children questioned, made mistakes, readjusted and tested their assumptions. When given stimuli such as visits, radio, television and so on, the 'what', 'why' and 'how' questions of older children, in both team and individual studies, began to produce a readiness for more regulated lessons. This, after all, is how science itself has developed over hundreds of years, as human curiosity, dissatisfied with purely philosophical explanations, has inspired questions and investigations in the real world.

Several teachers asked for help in more difficult areas such as measurement and recording and how to incorporate these tasks within the pattern of discoveries and finding solutions to immediate needs. We tried to warn teachers that turning investigations into an orthodox lesson can quickly destroy progress, especially in schools which already operated on a more rigid regime. We argued that a pre-planned programme for 8–10 year olds is more productive if it includes some free choice of activity. And the message got across – all the teachers involved noted an overall improvement in attitudes to work.

I was able to continue working with the Froebel Foundation and the Association for Science Education in writing information booklets to support teachers on appropriate equipment and useful addresses, ideas for activities and how to develop these, as well as information books for children (e.g. the 'Clue Books for Natural History').

We achieved a great deal. When the first National Curriculum for Science was written in 1988, the Working Party at that time placed considerable emphasis on the importance of developing children's 'attitudes' in science education, attitudes such as curiosity, co-operation with others and perseverance, as well as sensitivity to living things. Although this emphasis was lost during the intervening years, it has crept back into the latest version of the National Curriculum (2000).

Nevertheless, we still have some way to go. We have a somewhat parochial, nationalistic view of education. Education for all children of all ages frequently fails to recognise the significance of children in the global community as an essential part of developing attitudes that will influence the future well-being of us all.

3 To see and admire; not harm or destroy

A short history of the School Natural Science Society

John Williams

John Williams has recently retired from Anglia Polytechnic University, where he was responsible for Design and Technology in the School of Education. He still lectures in science, technology and ICT and is a freelance author. He was the last Chairman of the School Natural Science Society.

For those of us who can remember the days before the National Curriculum, science probably did not feature very prominently in our primary schools. Whether we were pupils or teachers, or indeed both, it is likely that the only science we encountered was natural history, with the physical sciences nowhere to be seen. There were obvious exceptions. There have always been individual teachers who have welcomed new subjects and new ideas into the curriculum and, more importantly, seen them as an opportunity to enrich our children's experience.

Kate Hall must have been such a person. She was the curator of the Stepney Borough Museum at the beginning of the last century. For a long time, she had been interested in the direct observation of nature. Her museum displays included living specimens of plants and animals, a very innovative idea for the time. This was in London's East End, and one can only imagine the effect this must have had on children whose previous experience of these, if at all, would have been as stuffed or pressed specimens in books or glass cases.

The School Nature Study Union, 1903

At the time of Kate Hall, nature study was edging its way into the elementary school curriculum. However, for many teachers this was a new subject and, as has been the case in similar and more recent circumstances, they needed help, advice and resources. It was for this reason that the School Nature Study Union was formed in 1903, with Miss Hall as its first treasurer. Meetings were held in her museum at the Free Library, 77 High Street, Whitechapel. She enlisted the help of the Reverend Claude Hinscliff, Curate of St George-in-the-East, who became the society's first secretary.

There had always been a strong church connection. The museum itself was formed at the suggestion of the Vicar of St Paul's Church, The Rev. Dan Greatorex. Through his interest in the welfare of the sailors in his parish (near the docks), he had received many specimens of animals, plants and rocks. These formed the nucleus of the museum's collection. Miss Hall was also able to obtain funds towards the setting up of the society. In those days before corporate sponsorship, this was no mean feat, and one I envied when, many years later, I too was looking for sponsorship for the society.

The society prospered and for many years the museum was the venue for meetings, as well as a base for permanent exhibitions. From the beginning, the importance of studying living things in their environment was recognised, and to this end one of the society's first activities was a conference about school nature expeditions. Outdoor meetings had an important place in the society's programme, and teachers were taken on pond-dipping expeditions, and botanical and geological excursions to such places as Leith Hill, Effingham Common and Bookham in Surrey, and to Epping Forest in Essex.

The society's first publications were issued in 1905 and, by 1906, increasing numbers of children were being taught at the museum. As one local headmistress wrote:

Here the unspoiled child with its natural instincts of intense curiosity, habit of observation and keen love of question, guided by wise suggestion, may learn much for itself and is stimulated to acquire habits and interests which may be retained through life.

Maintaining the society

The museum stayed open for many years and even during the First World War it was seldom closed to the public. However, in the dark days of 1942, when most staff were occupied in war work, the local council had to arrange for its 'temporary' closure. It never reopened and the society never again had a permanent base. From then on it relied on the generosity of schools, colleges and local authorities to provide venues for its meetings and conferences. These were often freely donated to the society, or only a nominal charge was made. For many years, our committee meetings were held at County Hall in Central London until its closure in the 1980s. By this time schools were beginning to take control of their own budgets, which meant that the society had to pay the going rate.

In 1963, the society had widened its interests in order to include physical as well as biological science and had even changed its name to the School Natural Science Society (SNSS) to reflect this.

Valedictory: the demise of the society after 90 years

The society had always been a voluntary organisation. Its money had derived from the moderate membership fee, which had paid for the journal and other publications, but there was no other income. With the growth of interest in primary science, other organisations and publishing companies became involved with the development of primary science, none more so than the ASE itself. Maintaining the SNSS became very difficult. It was a truly amateur society, relying on the goodwill of its officers, not only for the day-to-day management, but to edit the journal, organise meetings and carry out the work of a national organisation. For at least a decade, the society's numbers had remained static whilst the costs had increased. The writing was on the wall. A decision was made to close down the society, and in the autumn of 1992 the final journal was published.

For nearly ninety years, the society had supported the teaching of science in elementary and primary schools. It had organised meetings and symposia which had been attended by hundreds of teachers. Its journal and other publications had world-wide distribution. It had some influence on the political scene, producing evidence for the Parliamentary Committee for the Arts, Science and Education. A proud record!

Journal of the School Natural Science Society

Throughout the life of the society, many people had contributed their time and energy to the work of the SNSS. They cannot all be named here, nor would they wish to be, but they include school managers and class teachers, the generals and the foot soldiers. All gave their time freely and without qualification. Some were well known. In 1978, HRH The Duke of Edinburgh became our President and later our Patron. Sir David Attenborough, Sir Peter Scott, Dr Jonathan Miller and Professor Heinz Wolff were all presidents at one time or another. Famous or not, whoever they were, their names are recorded in the journals and minutes of the society. These are now housed in the Brotherton Library in the University of Leeds, where future researchers will recognise the society's contribution to science education.

In writing this, I have used the minutes and articles from the society's meetings and journals. The society used to print its motto at the head of all its publications. It makes a fitting epitaph and motto for the start of a new, and hopefully an environmentally friendly, twenty-first century:

To see and admire; not harm or destroy.

If any readers have in their possession SNSS material, journals or correspondence, which they would like to donate to the archive collection, it would be greatly appreciated. John Williams can be contacted via the ASE, or material can be sent directly to the Brotherton Library at the University of Leeds.

4 Primary science in the 1950s and 1960s

Margaret Collis

Science takes hold in primary schools and the ASE Primary Committee is born

Margaret Collis worked as a teacher, lecturer and HM Inspector. She was a founder member, and later Chair, of the ASE Primary Science Sub-Committee and in the vanguard of changes in the late 1950s and early 1960s which influenced the development from nature study to the broader science curriculum of today with its increasing emphasis on scientific skills. These early initiatives also prompted the development of the Nuffield Junior Science Project. Later, Margaret and the Primary Science Sub-Committee team wrote innovative publications for primary science which were to influence good practice all around the country.

In many colleges of education in the 1950s and early 1960s science training for primary school teachers was limited to biology. Consequently much of the work in primary schools was of a biological nature. Many schools possessed class sets of natural history books and these were used to read about science instead of doing science. Sometimes more old-fashioned books were still in use, such as *Stories for little listeners – a teacher's book of stories for use in connection with nature and conversation lessons*. These stories were often of a sentimental nature. They also conveyed false impressions when the plants and creatures indulged in imaginary conversations. For example, in *Tales of the wild folk: Wanda the wood ant*, the text

25

reads: '*We did not grow from seeds,*' *said a pink hyacinth to the daffodil.* '*We grew from bulbs which the farmer planted last October.*'

Teachers providing children with facilities for carrying out their own investigations in the classroom or school grounds, or encouraging outdoor exploration further afield, were in the minority. Only one organisation had tried to support primary teachers in this area: the School Natural Science Society (formerly the School Nature Study Union). This society had, from the early years of the century, through its publications and exhibitions, consistently encouraged and helped teachers to carry out investigations of natural phenomena with primary children. The ASE at this time (or its forerunners) was for secondary teachers and had no primary members.

The groundswell of interest in primary science

From 1955 to 1959 I was a member of the Derbyshire Advisory Service and, as a former teacher and lecturer in biology and health education, was very interested in encouraging the development of science in the primary schools in my area. I also enjoyed providing courses in field studies to the Local Education Authority in-service training programme.

At that time, HMI Edith Biggs was assigned to the Derbyshire area and we met when she visited an evening course in science that I was providing for teachers in South Derbyshire. Edith's enthusiasm for developments in primary school mathematics, and my enthusiasm for developments in science, led us to enjoy co-operating and working together whenever opportunities occurred. It was either at the end of 1958 or in January 1959 that Edith told me she was a member of a working party of HMIs

---

25 years ago

As a science (+ maths + IT) co-ordinator, I went to a maths and science conference in South London. The conference facilities were being shared with the Catholic Ladies Convention. Returning from the student bar with fellow teachers, after the first hard day's work, I fell into step with a little old lady, whom I assumed to be a 'Catholic Lady'.

'*Are you having a nice time?*', I asked, speaking loudly in case she was hard of hearing. '*Yes, thank you,*' she said, '*are you?*' I talked non-stop about the important work we were doing in primary maths and science until we parted amicably at the door of the Hall of Residence.

It was only then that my fellow teachers around me collapsed in hysterical laughter. '*Do you know who that was?*' they asked. '*A Catholic Lady?*' I replied tentatively. '*THAT was Edith Biggs! HMI! The keynote speaker tomorrow! The maths guru!*'

I was mortified. My presumptions about elderly ladies and Catholic Ladies in particular were grossly exposed.

The following morning I saw Edith Biggs and took my breakfast across to eat with her, along with some humble pie. She cut my apologies short: she had been amused by the incident and forgave me. She was a great woman: not only a formative influence on primary mathematics and science but courteous, considerate and good-humoured too. And I learnt a big lesson.

Max de Bóo

---

considering the teaching of science in primary schools. She asked me if I would lend her some examples of children's work in science, from the collection I used for in-service training, to serve with that collected by other HMIs as a basis for discussion at the next meeting of the Ministry of Education working party. I was very pleased to do this.

A Ministry of Education course

The discussions at the Ministry of Education resulted in a high-level course, in July 1959, 'Science in Primary Schools', at the Maria Asumpta College of Education (now closed). The organising team comprised John Goldsmith HMI (course leader), Miss M. Nicholls HMI (primary education), Gwyneth Jones HMI (biology), Len Ennever HMI (physical science) and Edith Biggs HMI (mathematics).

The strength and expertise of the course team was an indication of the importance Her Majesty's Inspectors attached to the development of primary science education. Members of the course – about 30 to 40 in number – came by invitation. They were all people known to be actively concerned with developments in science teaching, including, for example: Albert James from Rachel Macmillan College of Education, author of a very successful series of books in natural science; Dr Laybourn, Manchester LEA Inspectorate and Mr Bailey, Manchester Metropolitan University, joint authors of a much used and valued book on science experiments in secondary schools; John Bartle, Inspector of Education, Kent, with responsibility for science; Frank Blackwell, Headmaster of Newington Primary School, Ramsgate; Mr W. Rudge, Headmaster of Beaver Green Primary School in Ashford, Kent; a Headmistress of a one-teacher primary school in Yorkshire where work of distinction was in progress; and teachers that I brought from two South Derbyshire primary schools. I cannot recall all the delegates but it was an impressive course list.

All the course members were asked to provide examples of interesting work in science that had been developed in their own areas. This was set out as an exhibition of good current work in primary schools and was used as a basis for discussion. I provided a display of work that had arisen from studies of an area of waste ground in Swadlincote, South Derbyshire (a mining and pottery area).

In his opening address to the course, John Goldsmith referred to a study of children's questions. While this revealed much interest in plants and animals, it also showed that children were curious about many physical phenomena and wanted to know more about them. Therefore, there was strong justification for a broader programme of scientific experiences for primary school children. Miss Nicholls spoke about general primary school practice. Len Ennever's focus was elementary electricity as an illustration of some of the physical science that should have a place in primary school programmes. Gwyneth Jones described the exciting first-hand investigations into birds that she had seen in school and Edith Biggs convinced us that scientific investigations also gave children excellent opportunities to learn and apply mathematics.

Discussions included classroom organisation – a necessary consideration if we were to advocate the importance of children's own practical investigations, in other words, 'doing science'. By the end of this meeting we were all agreed that we would 'spread the gospel' on return to our own areas.

Further developments

In the months following the Ministry course, it became obvious that interest in primary school science was increasing rapidly:

• A conference was organised by the British Association for the Advancement of Science. The speakers included Dr Laybourn and Frank Blackwell, members of the initial Ministry course.

• The School Nature Study Union became The School Natural Science Society (SNSS) and discussions between members of its executive committee, concerned with broadening its objectives, were lively and prolonged.

• Books on primary school science were written by Albert James and Maurice Branson (Adviser for Rural Studies in Essex and an ASE member) and snapped up in large numbers by the teaching profession.

• The BBC scheduled programmes for science in primary schools in its Education Service. Of course, there was some confusion too. As with any new and interesting development, people were anxious to 'jump on the bandwagon' without really understanding it. Some teachers expressed enthusiasm for teaching science instead of nature study, without realising that the study of nature can involve both living and non-living things.

In September of that year (1959), following the Ministry course, I moved from Derbyshire to Kent, becoming an Inspector of Education. My particular concerns were primary education and science, and responsibility for advising in schools of the Medway and Folkestone Divisions in the county. By now, there was great activity around the country. A few years later (1963), at a science meeting in London (organised by ASE or the Froebel Foundation), I met an active member of ASE, Don Marchant (Kesteven College of Education). Don had just been appointed to chair a new ASE group committed to developing primary science teaching; he invited me to join that group, known then as the Primary Science Sub-Committee of the ASE Education Committee.

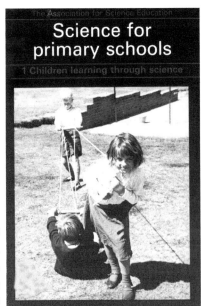

One of the early publications of the ASE Primary Science Sub-Committee, *Science for Primary Schools: 1 Children learning through science* (John Murray, 1966)

The ASE Primary Science Sub-Committee

The members of the sub-committee were a prestigious group, many of whom you will meet elsewhere in this book. They included Don Marchant (Chair), Eric Breeze (secondary school science teacher and ASE Officer), Albert James, Maurice Branson, Ron Wastnedge (Kesteven College of Education), Gwen Allen (Froebel Educational Institute, Roehampton), N. F. Newbury (Lancashire LEA and consultant to the BBC primary science programmes), myself and one or two others. We also benefited from the wisdom of Gwyneth Jones HMI and Len Ennever HMI, who attended in an advisory capacity.

The first discussions of this sub-committee focused on the formulation of a policy statement. In subsequent meetings, group members worked on the production of three booklets to help primary school teachers (recently updated):

- Descriptions of good practice in science observed in primary schools.
- A list of books we could recommend for primary school science.
- Apparatus and equipment valuable in primary school science.

A fourth booklet was produced with the BBC on making effective use of school broadcasts.

It was a very hectic time! Members of this sub-committee were very active in contributing to ASE Regional Meetings and in-service courses of Local Education Authorities and Institutes of Education. At the Annual Meeting of the ASE in Cambridge, 1966, Maurice Branson and I set up the first small exhibition of work from primary schools. Gwen Allen wrote an article on science in primary education that broke new ground when it was accepted for publication in the ASE journal, *The School Science Review*. (This was the only ASE journal then – written for the members, who were still mostly secondary.)

Influencing the Nuffield Science initiative

At an early stage in the ASE developments described above, Albert James, Len Ennever and I were invited with others to a meeting at Nuffield House. Money was to be made available for Nuffield projects to help forward science teaching. We were asked to make a case for some of this money to finance a project on primary school science. This project was agreed and Ron Wastnedge became its Director. Although this meant him leaving the ASE Primary Science Sub-Committee to concentrate on the new development, it worked to everyone's advantage as the work of the ASE and Nuffield Science teams developed along parallel lines with much co-operation between the two groups.

During the last years of Don Marchant's chairmanship of the ASE Primary Science Sub-Committee, middle schools began to appear, some covering the age range 8–12 years, others 9–13 years. Should the sub-committee try to address the concerns of these schools? If so, how? The problem was unresolved when Don Marchant retired in 1971 and I was invited to become the new Chair. I was also encouraged to recruit new members of the group.

Chairing the Primary Science Sub-Committee

Along with changes in membership, there were changes in meeting place. Until that time, we had met in London at the Mary Ward Centre. I suggested that it was more fitting for our meetings to take place at ASE headquarters in Hatfield and it was there that we were joined by Audrey Randall (Headmistress of Brookland County Infants School, Cheshunt), Roger Harris (Headmaster of Water Mill Primary School, Selly Oak, Birmingham), Roy Richards (Principal Lecturer in Education, Goldsmiths College), and Doug Kincaid (Advisory Teacher for Science, Berkshire). A year later we were joined by Dr Helen Rapson, subsequently Editor of *ASE Primary Science*.

By this time there were more publications on primary science. We did not want to reinvent the wheel so we looked around for areas that had not received attention. The first of these was support for headteachers. In many schools headteachers were anxious to have good science programmes in the curriculum but often did not become personally involved. So we wrote *The role of the Headteacher* (1974) to help improve this situation. The second book, *A post of responsibility* (1976), was designed to help teachers holding graded posts in primary science – the first of its kind for science. These sold out pretty quickly and were later revised, largely by Helen Rapson, to take account of the continuing new developments. Helen also began to edit the broadsheet *ASE Primary Science*, launched in 1980, to offer good examples of children's work collected from primary schools. The broadsheet was bought in large numbers by Local Education Authority Advisers who distributed it to schools: the message was being transmitted!

In addition, in our determination to promote the development of primary science and the role of the ASE, we produced exhibition material explaining the work of the sub-committee, responded to a host of enquiries, gave in-service courses around the country and talks at ASE Regional and Annual Meetings.

We decided to publish teaching materials to support aspects of physical science at a time when there was a national concern over the conservation of energy. We produced three best-selling booklets: *Moving things*; *Burning, warmth and sunlight*; and *Working with electricity*. Writing took time and thought (remember we all had full-time jobs elsewhere). We adopted a method whereby one member of the group wrote the first draft; this was then studied by the whole group, modifications suggested and a revised draft then written. It was a lengthy process but valuable: the refereeing process is a recognised strategy to iron out confusion and mistakes before final publication, and monitor issues such as health and safety, equal opportunities and access to science for all. This same process is still used for any material that is brought to the ASE for publication under its logo.

This sub-committee functioned until 1979 before achieving the status of a full ASE Committee. Some secondary members clearly doubted that the primary members meant business and were here to stay! Unfortunately, sub-committee status meant that during all those years, we were not allocated a permanent secretary (a staff member of ASE HQ). We took it in turns to record the minutes of the meetings and passed these on (when we retired from the sub-committee) to Cathy Wilson (then of ASE, now Institute of Physics) as a full record of our work.

It would be difficult to even imagine the ASE nowadays without the involvement of the primary membership. The Association had been a society of secondary and tertiary teachers, mostly male, for its first 60 years. Once primary members joined, the focus of the Association had to change and expand – a good thing for any organisation. ASE would never be the same again. By the end of the century (1998–1999), Council's choice for the prestigious post of Chair of the whole Association was not only a woman, but a primary member, Rosemary Feasey! Primary science had definitely arrived!

The joys of teaching

Advice to teachers: know when to quit

We are going to learn today about different types of fire. What sorts of fires are there at home?

Please miss, we've got a gas fire in our house.

Good, what does a gas fire use?

Gas, miss.

Good. Any more?

We've got an electric fire.

Yes, and what does it use?

Electricity.

Good. Any more?

We've got a coal fire.

Good, and what does it use?

Coal.

Good. Any more?

We've got a bonfire.

Good, and what does ...

If you can keep your head, when .....

The temperature in the room was rising rapidly, such was the heat of discussion on a question of change in the organisation's practices.

One side, advocating change, argued that their proposals, far from being airy-fairy notions, were very similar to practices in operation elsewhere.

The other side, in a momentary lapse of concentration, responded, *'It's all very well for you to provide evidence that these ideas work in practice, but do they work in theory?'*

Going to school (or not)

Son: *I don't want to go to school today. Nobody likes me. The teachers hate me and the pupils hate me. And I can't do the work.*

Mother: *I'm sure it's not as bad as that. You must go. Besides, you are the headteacher.*

Attendance Officer: *Can I speak to Darren's father, please?*

Deep voice: *This is my father speaking.*

Girl, aged 5, about to start school: *I don't want to go to school. Why do I have to go?*

Mother: *You have to go to school until you are 16.*

Girl (in floods of tears): *You will remember to come back for me when I'm 16.*

Food for thought

The best of teaching is directed at making the teacher redundant. If not, the learner is forever condemned to dependence.

Worthwhile education is always experimental. If it is not, it denies the individuality of the learner.

Neville Evans

From *Humour, muse, enterprise* (1998) published by The Leonard Cheshire Homes and Ty Hafan, The Children's Hospice in Wales.

5 From nature study to environmental studies ∞

Nicky Souter

Recollections and a short history of primary science in Scotland

Nicky Souter has taught in the University of Strathclyde, Faculty of Education (formerly Jordanhill College), since 1990. Teaching priorities have been towards biology, science, environmental education and health education across the full range of undergraduate and postgraduate courses. He also has considerable experience of teaching in secondary schools and of curriculum design and implementation through various bodies in Scotland such as SCCC and SEB. He has contributed to a range of publications including a chapter in the recently published definitive text on Scottish education, as well as editing and co-authoring *Standard grade science* for Hodder and Stoughton. Professional interests include being a member of the Institute of Biology and of course the Association for Science Education. He is active locally, regionally and nationally within ASE. His lifetime sporting passion is currently being applied to getting his golf handicap to a respectable level!

'Lesley Brown, where are you?'

It must have been during Autumn 1959 and we children were in Primary 4. Please do not ask me to prove it – my wife says that I have a remarkable capability for recollecting trivial and irrelevant details. My mother, who is even more direct, often declares that I have a 'vivid imagination'. The evidence is derived from each of the following: the task – drawing winter leaves and trees; the location – a classroom on the lower floor of the south side of the old primary school nearest to the 'Fern Avenue' gate; and the year – just before we were decanted to the 'Annexe'. We had been taken to the playground, adorned with Burberrys (i.e. coats – for the uninitiated), hats and scarves (to keep out the 'chill'), to collect some leaves that had blown on to the concrete school surrounds. I do remember that it was a glorious afternoon: it was the afternoon since the mornings were always taken up with the priority tasks of reading, writing and 'doing' sums. Afternoons were used for handwork, art, music, 'drill' (later promoted to physical education), history, geography and nature study. Actually, if it was nature study, it was probably a Thursday! (Data not available!)

Lesley Brown was the pretty, blonde girl with a mole on her cheek who lived down 'my' road. Lesley could draw the most amazing trees! At a time when most of us were scribbling something that looked like a stick with straw on top, Lesley's trees had shape, scale, shading and branching with a grandeur that made her drawings look just like the real thing. I guess that we must have been 'doing' nature study. During that period, objects appeared at frequent intervals: the teacher would invite us to collect pussy-willow catkins and tadpoles in spring; we would grow bulbs in glass jars; make collections of seeds and berries in the autumn and feathers at any time of the year. We roamed around the neighbourhood searching for pond life, birds' pellets and animal tracks. I wonder how many of today's children encounter such a rich experience of their local environment?

Did my experience reflect the intentions of the curriculum planners of the day who had suggested in a 1950 Memorandum (Scottish Education Department, 1950) that the primary curriculum should include nature study and that it should include scientific activities such as those above?

Conditions prevailing in the nineteenth century

Let's return to the beginning. For many reasons the Education Act of 1872 is a useful starting point. Schools had existed for some time in Scotland. For example, the Ayr Academy website claims, 'We have been here for 750 years...', but there is no definite date given as to when teaching began, although it is thought it was sometime before 1233. The famous Scottish poet, Robert Burns, was enrolled by his father in 1773 to 'perfect his grammar'. In *A short history of Craigie Primary School* in Perth (Fothergill, 1982), it is reported that practices in the school following the 1872 Education Act reflected the public profile of science at that time. The inspectors commended the pupils' curriculum, which included botany and physical geography. However, it was noted that in May 1876, the headteacher, Mr Berkeley, introduced magnetism and electricity. Berkeley was reported as having *'an outstanding knowledge and enthusiasm for botany and mycology'* and as being an active member of the Perthshire Society of Natural Science, of which he was president in 1907.

According to Cooper (1973) the conditions in those early elementary schools were dependent on factors such as the school roll and the prosperity of the community. Although the 1872 Act had made education compulsory for children between 5 and 13 years of age, it did not make it free. Each school board set the fees that were to be approved and which were not permitted to exceed 9d per week, the equivalent of 4 pence today. Although that may sound like a bargain, it is important to remember that in the 1870s miners earned between 80 and 90 pence per week (and often had several children to support and send to school).

Large numbers of children and low earnings characterised many schools and this must have influenced basic resourcing within the school. The 1881 log book of the Beckford Street School, Hamilton, reported *'the writing had to be dispensed with this afternoon as the ink was frozen. Great mortality in my aquarium; the stickleback is embedded in a solid lump of ice'*. Whilst it is worth noting that nature study of sorts was taking place, possibly by direct observation of living things in the classroom, it is somewhat disturbing that the livestock met such an unhappy demise. One wonders what temperature the children had to endure!

At the turn of the century, HM Inspectors had often reported 'highly commended' infant class teaching which included nature talks. Collins (1965) reports that, according to the log book of Low Water School in Hamilton, object lessons were often supported with artefacts such as animal fur, silkworm cocoons, feathers, sponges, whalebone, gold, silver, coal, salt, paper and gutta-percha. Despite these object lessons being resourced with potentially stimulating starting materials, the emphasis appears largely to have been on committing facts to memory.

The predominance of nature study

Walter Hulmes (1983) reminds us that science was probably the leading concept of the nineteenth century and this influenced social, cultural and philosophical life during the Victorian years. It is not surprising therefore that science should appear in the school curriculum following the 1872 Act. What is, perhaps, surprising is that the experience of science was principally restricted to the life sciences encapsulated within nature study; disappointingly, the physical sciences did not secure a firm foothold. Had this not been so, the issues associated with teachers' confidence might have been different.

A further confounding factor during the establishment of the early curriculum was the vociferous debate that took place following the publication of the *Origin of Species*. During the Victorian era, Scotland was influenced by, and participated in, the ideology of science. The contributions of Kelvin, Simpson, Lyell, Clerk-Maxwell, Dewar and many others are a testimony to this. The Presbyterian Church, however, represented a substantial focus of hostility towards science. Walter Hulmes says *'evolutionary biology, … by challenging the doctrine of "special creation" for man, seemed to pose a clear threat to biblical authority and religious orthodoxy'*.

Science teaching in primary school appears to have continued in much the same way from the Victorian period until the post-war education reforms. It may be a selective or ageing memory, but I cannot recall any physical science activities at all in my own education in the 1950s and 60s. If this is a common experience, then we should not express surprise that Harlen, Holroyd and Byrne (1995) reported that primary teachers were *'less confident about teaching science and technology than about almost all other curriculum areas'*. Teachers were *'rather more confident about "Living things and the processes of life" and "Earth and space" than about "Energy and forces"…'*

Harlen's findings had been heralded in a small ASE investigation (ASE, Scotland, 1990) in the upper primary school which surveyed practice in P6 and P7. Analysis of a questionnaire administered to 90 headteachers and Primary 6/7 teachers revealed that the majority of primary staff had no particular expertise in science, and that those who did had a wide range of experience. Almost half the main areas of science taught were derived from topics of a biological nature. They also found that pupils were likely to spend more time on science during the later stages of primary school.

Paul Black suggested in Adams (1985) that the practice of nature study was widespread and that before the Oxford Primary Science and Nuffield Junior Science Projects started in the 1960s, *'primary school science was mainly confined to nature study of which a leading educator [uncited] said "nature too seldom comes into the work and too often study is the last thing thought of ".'* This observation, although referring to the situation in England, may equally well have applied to the Scottish curriculum.

The initial Scottish report on primary education (Scottish Education Department, 1946) was written during the immediate post-war period. It makes interesting, almost Churchillian reading: *'We have faced unpleasant realities without flinching. We have been discovered to be tougher than others supposed or even we ourselves imagined. In the great crisis we have so upheld international standards as to secure worldwide respect and a share in the moral leadership of nations.'* This report described fundamental subjects and included nature study alongside geography and history. This was justified since *'they represent the desire and the need of the child to know his world'*. The earlier object lessons and the use of artefacts were coupled with the emergent view on child-centredness, such that *'the pupil will be thrilled to have a personal stake or interest in the discussion, and his crude but eager story may, through training, become a more scientific and formal statement'*. (Pupils were referred to as 'he' and the teacher as 'she' throughout this report.) This report was formalised in the 1950 Memorandum (Scottish Education Department, 1950) and the aims of nature study were described in the following way:

a) To train the child in careful observation.

b) To impart some knowledge of familiar natural phenomena.

c) To foster an appreciation of nature.

d) To indicate in a simple fashion, the interdependence of men, animals and plants and their dependence on physical conditions.

e) To encourage a humane attitude towards living things and to counteract any inclination towards wanton destruction.

f) To provide valuable leisure-time interest.

The Memorandum left the school to determine its own scheme of work dependent upon the school's environment. At upper primary the Memorandum suggested the following topics:

Task 1: Colour and nature

a) adaptation of general structure to mode of life

b) suitability of particular structures for their purpose

c) protective devices in plants and animals.

Science as integrated into the curriculum

John Blackie's general description, *Inside the primary school* (Blackie, 1967), indicates that topic approaches were being used and had the advantage of pursuing children's curiosity. He confirms that, until that time, the only science taught in primary schools had been natural history, or nature study, as it was called in the timetables. John Blackie suggested that *'the aim of teaching science in a primary school is*

Primary children in Scotland taking measurements for science in the playground in 1965 (from *Primary Education in Scotland*, Scottish Education Department/HMSO, 1965. Crown Copyright)

not really to lay the foundations of scientific knowledge, still less to offer elementary introductions to different sciences'. He suggested that those matters which interested children could contribute to general education, and in doing so he suggested an enquiry methodology as *'[teachers] found out not only how it works but what questions it is sensible to ask [children] and how to find the answers and check their accuracy'.* John Blackie also noted the interdependence of curricular areas, emphasising the requirement for mathematics skills.

The 1950 Scottish Memorandum was replaced in 1965 (Scottish Education Department, 1965). This paper introduced new curriculum areas and recommended integrated approaches: *'It cannot be too strongly stressed that education is concerned as much with the personal development of the child as the teaching of subjects.'* In recognising this, the Scottish Education Department created the curriculum area of 'environmental studies' which incorporated history, geography and science. Some exemplification was given, for example topics on weather, transport, clothing and local studies for junior school, and the local area, homeland, and the remainder of the world for upper primary.

Environmental studies was justified on the grounds that *'they all in some degree involve activities which are grounded in the child's observation and investigation of his surroundings'* and this could foster *'in the child the desire to know more about the world around him and train him in the skills he needs to interpret it'.* Progression was supplied within the primary school where *'more systematic subject studies'* would take place. The concept of 'centres of interest' is embedded within the notion of environmental studies as outlined in 1965 and suggests that *'this does not imply a total separation into subjects at these stages, nor that each will receive the same amount of attention and time each week, or even each month ... the teacher should [choose how] to develop aspects of current interest, and the emphasis will change from time to time according to the centre of interest and the extent to which subjects are co-ordinated. A balance, however, should be aimed at over a period of time, possibly a term.'*

The question of confidence

HM Inspectors of schools reported in 1980 (Scottish Education Department, 1980) on learning and teaching in Scottish primary schools. With some disappointment, they noted that there were problems with environmental studies. They noted (paragraph 4.3) that *'so little time was given to environmental studies by one in five P4 teachers and one in ten P7 teachers that no judgements about their work could be made'*. While noting these concerns on overall provision for environmental studies, they pointed out that *'science fared badly, with 60% of all teachers giving it little, if any, place in their curriculum'*. The Inspectors also noted that the overwhelming priority was given to the transmission of knowledge and facts. The performance of children when they attempted to assess general scientific knowledge provided evidence that little science was being taught. They concluded that *'the extent to which science is neglected, especially at the P7 stage, is a very real concern ... the whole area of environmental studies requires to be reviewed ... What seems to be required is enough support to give teachers confidence, security, and the conviction that what they are being asked to do is practicable, given a reasonable amount of time and effort ... As a matter of priority, something has to be done for them in science; but first it will be necessary to assess what schools can reasonably be expected to achieve.'*

Although the priority was clearly defined for curriculum reform and development (let alone support for teachers), assessment guidelines for environmental studies did not appear until 1993. These included science with social subjects, information and communication technology and health education. Assessing these, transfer of information to secondary schools and the nature of environmental studies have continued to present teachers with problems. Teachers in both sectors have difficulty in planning appropriate, progressive programmes for experimental and investigative science or the development of informed attitudes. The work goes on to 'get it right' for children, teachers and the future within the constraints imposed from above.

And what of Lesley Brown?

We both studied biology at Glasgow University, graduated in 1972 and proceeded directly to teacher training courses – secondary for me and primary for Lesley. She married a zoology lecturer and the last I heard was that Lesley taught her own and other children at home in a liberalised manner. Did those children draw winter trees with the same skill as she had in the 1950s? What scientific attitudes and values have they adopted? Have the new curricula with their explicit specification of syllabus, content and skills removed rather than promoted the potential for enquiry and exploration? Do the tightly specified targets, outcomes and strands support or hinder effective teaching? Do they support learning or constrain enquiry? Do they permit investigative approaches to be pursued with vigour and enthusiasm by learners in response to their needs, interests and level of attainment or do they provide a straitjacket which binds future creativity, sensitivity and curiosity?

Curriculum planners and politicians take note!

References

Adams, F. (1985) *Science and computers in primary education: a report of the educational research workshop held in Edinburgh (Scotland), 3–6 September 1984*. Edinburgh: SCRE (Scottish Council for Research in Education).

ASE (Scotland) (1990) *An investigation into science in the upper primary school*. ASE (Scottish Region).

Blackie, J. (1967) *Inside the primary school*. London: HMSO.

Collins, C. (1965) The development of education in Hamilton with particular reference to the period of the school boards, 1872–1918. Unpublished BEd thesis, University of Glasgow.

Cooper, S. (1973) *The 1872 Education Act in Lanarkshire*. Hamilton: Hamilton College of Education.

Fothergill, R. (1982) *A short history of Craigie Primary School*. Perth: Craigie Primary School.

Harlen, W., Holroyd, C. and Byrne, M. (1995) *Confidence and understanding in teaching science and technology in primary schools*. Edinburgh: SCRE (Scottish Council for Research in Education).

Hulmes, W. (1983) *Scottish culture and Scottish education 1800–1980*. Edinburgh: John Donald.

Scottish Education Department (1946) *Primary Education – a report of the Advisory Council on Education in Scotland*. Edinburgh: HMSO.

Scottish Education Department (1950) *The primary school in Scotland: a memorandum on the curriculum*. Edinburgh: HMSO.

Scottish Education Department (1965) *Primary education in Scotland*. Edinburgh: HMSO.

Scottish Education Department (1980) *Learning and teaching in Primary 4 and Primary 7*. Edinburgh: HMSO.

Scottish Education Department (1993) *Environmental Studies: curriculum and assessment guidelines in Scotland*. Edinburgh: Scottish Office Education Dept.

6 A revolutionary project

Ron Wastnedge

The Nuffield Junior Science Teaching Project, 1964–1966

Ron Wastnedge taught science in schools and colleges for many years. He was a founder member of the ASE Primary Science Sub-Committee and President of the School Natural Science Society (SNSS). He worked on many overseas in-service projects developing primary teachers' understanding of science education, such as the Wave Hill Project in New York (teachers working in the Bronx) and in Canada (Ontario and New Brunswick). He was the Director of the Nuffield Junior Science Teaching Project from 1964 to 1966, working with teachers around the country, writing supporting books and other materials. He was an HMI from 1966 until 1981; during this time he was involved with the writing of the influential Government document *Science 5–16: a statement of policy*, the primary survey, and producing ASE-validated certificated courses in primary science. He worked extensively and enthusiastically with teachers and HE tutors on ITE and INSET courses. He is currently working on improving his less-than-satisfactory (level 3?) golf handicap.

Material for this chapter has been taken from Goodwin, A. and Wastnedge, E. R. (1995) The Nuffield Junior Science Teaching Project (Jan. 1964 – Dec. 1966), *Didsbury IDEAS*, **5**(3), with additional material supplied by Ron Wastnedge. Alan Goodwin teaches in the Department of Sciences Education, Manchester Metropolitan University.

Editors' note

This contribution is given prominence because the Nuffield Junior Science Teaching Project, its Director, Ron Wastnedge, the project team and collaborating teachers had such an influence on the evolution of primary science education. Of all projects, it was the one that placed the problems and solutions fairly and squarely with class teachers and acted upon their responses. Norman Booth (one of the original 'Nuffield' teachers, later headteacher, then HMI) once said, *'It was the most teacher- and child-based project of them all.'*

The Nuffield Junior Science team were the ones who pressed for the setting up of teachers' centres, until then a rarity or completely unknown. The project influenced teachers' attitudes towards their own professionalism, towards group work in science and the emphasis on scientific enquiry skills or processes. The project was the stimulus and springboard for further initiatives, such as Science 5/13, and it influenced the Inspectorate in the questions chosen for their primary survey (1975). The Inspectorate was positive and supportive of the project's ideas: Jim Rose HMI and Ron Wastnedge, then HMI, prepared the consultative document *Science education in schools* (HMSO, 1982); they, and Edith Biggs, Norman Booth and Len Ennever, all contributed to the Government document *Science 5–16: a statement of policy* (HMSO, March 1985).

The Junior Science Project informed and inspired secondary school science, as well as teaching and learning approaches adopted overseas in the US, Canada and Africa.

Norman Booth HMI said, *'Without Nuffield Junior Science there would have been no National Curriculum.'* It is clear that the project was innovative in curriculum development and showed the positive benefits of children's learning in science. Whatever the merits or demerits of subsequent statutory documentation, everyone now assumes that children have an entitlement to a 'good' science education.

After the war

To understand the Nuffield Projects in general and the Junior Science Teaching Project in particular – why they operated as they did, why indeed they happened at all – we must appreciate the conditions existing in schools after the war ended in 1945.

Throughout the war, there had been massive conscription of young men and women into various kinds of war service. After six years of war, most schools had no teachers with any science training, and were starved of books and equipment. A legacy from pre-war days was that science was actually timetabled and taught only in the secondary sector and then only in grammar and public schools (secondary modern schools were not proposed until the 1944 Education Act, and anyone not winning a scholarship to a grammar school continued to attend an elementary school up to the age of 14), with the result that it was only those schools which had the specialist accommodation and equipment needed for practical science. Consequently, they were the schools which attracted qualified science graduate teachers.

The shortage of scientifically qualified staff, even in grammar schools, meant that many boys and girls (especially girls) passed through a system offering limited, mostly unbalanced, science. Some, again especially girls, studied some science for as few as two years out of five. The knock-on effect of all this was smaller science sixth-forms, fewer science graduates, and fewer trainee science teachers. And the situation was exacerbated by the fact that industry, trying to re-establish itself on a peace-time basis, offered salaries and working conditions considerably better than those offered to teachers.

The picture in secondary schools was a depressing one, with an emphasis on the learning of facts, a lack of practical work, and certainly of the scientific process. What was offered was characterised as 'chalk and talk' science, with practical work being described and often not even demonstrated by the teacher, let alone performed by pupils.

The picture in primary schools was, if possible, even more daunting. Although most primary school timetables included nature study, it was rarely given more than 20 or 30 minutes each week, and could easily be avoided by any teacher who felt inadequate to deal with it. Mostly, when taught, it comprised reading and copying chapters or illustrations from textbooks. Classroom nature tables became the target for teachers' jokes about wilting horse-chestnut twigs and dying tadpoles. It was difficult to find evidence of the much-vaunted nature walk, even in rural schools, and especially in urban areas, where most of the nation's primary schools were to be found.

One has sympathy for the teachers, whose plight was made more extreme by the pressures imposed by the newly devised 11+ examination, and the large class sizes. The post-war baby boom was working its way through the system, and classes of 50 or more children were the primary school norm rather than the exception. Suitable space for practical working and for storing equipment, if there was any, was severely limited by the numbers of double iron desks with sloping tops crammed into the available space. In any case, teachers had rarely, if ever, experienced or considered the possible techniques of organising practical work with their pupils.

An important, natural, and predictable response of teachers to their personal lack of scientific background, was to imitate some vaguely remembered role model. Often this would be a sixth-form or college teacher. The outcome was a tendency for teachers to stand in front of classes, lecture, and to expect written work in the passive voice.

Growing enthusiasm for practical primary science

Despite these depressing circumstances, there were still schools where dedicated, competent or gifted teachers helped children to learn and, what is more, to enjoy learning science with understanding. Scattered through the country were individuals and groups of people who were determinedly searching for something better.

For instance, by the 1950s many teachers recognised that 'nature' included a physical as well as a biological component, and that this fact should be reflected in school nature study. Ironically, this broadening of the concept of nature study presented a further, enormous problem to those teachers, the majority of whom had never studied physical science at school or at college and whose only recourse was to very elementary, sometimes unclear textbooks. An outstanding example was a teacher of 7-year-olds who actually relied upon Ladybird books, written for young children, for her background knowledge of science. She achieved outstanding success, but this is not to be recommended as a role model for the average teacher!

In parallel with this thinking ran the idea that practical investigation was what science was really all about, especially when performed by the children themselves. This was, of course, a laudable recognition that first-hand, concrete experience is essential for young children's learning, but it was also difficult to achieve in a world of overcrowded and ill-equipped classrooms. In any case, scientific equipment was very difficult to obtain, and was prohibitively expensive for most primary schools.

The answer was to use everyday, commonplace materials: jam-jars were substituted for beakers, and spirit burners were made from ink bottles with strips of cloth pushed through holes in the metal tops. This technique of building up a stock of 'make do and mend' equipment became widespread, sometimes becoming almost a fetish.

We should not sneer at this use of everyday materials. Not only did it stimulate

41

considerable ingenuity but it also indicated to children that science was not something which could only be done by men in white coats, in specialist laboratories, using expensive apparatus. When used intelligently, it could also bring about real understanding. For instance, a child who makes a simple electrical switch from a piece of balsa, drawing pins and paper clips, is likely to understand the mechanism of the commercial article and its function in a circuit.

Gradually, people came to believe that science in primary schools has a nature and ethos of its own, a nature determined by the abilities and stages of intellectual development of individual children. It should not be 'watered-down' secondary science.

The general response to the situation

This refreshing, albeit limited, appraisal of science teaching in schools came at a time when other groups were seeking ways of initiating change. In the world of nursery and infant education, Marianne Parry in Bristol was encouraging teachers to observe children carefully and then to help them learn effectively, and similar attitudes were being encouraged elsewhere. The so-called 'integrated day' emerged – probably a misnomer for a curriculum undifferentiated in subject terms – as teachers learned more about child development and felt the need to break free from subject-dominated teaching.

Around 1963, the ASE became aware of the importance of science in primary education and established its primary sub-committee. Simultaneously, from Geneva appeared accounts of Piaget's work. Although these presented difficult reading, it was not long before more easily assimilated analyses and summaries appeared and, by the early 60s, it was not uncommon to find teachers on in-service courses discussing some of Piaget's ideas in relation to their own work in classrooms.

I also witnessed some exciting spontaneous science starting to happen such as the following example.

The science in a puddle!

One rainy morning in an infants school in the Midlands, the children arrived to find a pool of water in the entrance hall. It had dripped in through a leaky roof. Great excitement! A teacher wondered how much water there was. This provoked much discussion until, finally, a 7-year-old boy suggested a method of finding out.

He fetched a 1 litre jug from the classroom. Next, he counted the number of parquet blocks covered by the rainwater. He mopped up the water, dried the floor, and then poured a litre of water from his jug so that he could count the number of parquet blocks it covered. He could now calculate how much rainwater was there originally.

It would be wrong, however, to paint a picture of a sudden general upsurge in the quality of science teaching. For the most part, schools remained as they had been for decades. Secondary teaching continued in its old mode of memorising facts, with little practical work and virtually no enquiry. Primary schools continued to plod wearily through a nature study that had little to do with nature and virtually nothing to do with study.

Human nature also had a part to play, for human beings rarely welcome change. Their own limited experience of learning science left the majority of primary school teachers feeling inadequate and insecure. The thought of managing a class of young children working as individuals or in small groups, in overcrowded classrooms and with insufficient equipment and books, provoked many into 'putting up the shutters' against change.

Additionally, as was almost inevitable in such a huge profession, more and more teachers climbed aboard the integrated day bandwagon without considering its educational rationale. More and more classrooms drifted towards that relative chaos which provoked Sir Alec Clegg to liken it to a *'kind of permanent wet playtime'*. Unfortunately, these untoward developments did little to help the movement towards a flexible, child-focused system of education. Even today, the worst excesses of the 60s are being used as a cudgel with which to beat the teaching profession, with the very real danger that much of the good that was achieved will be undone, as the new traditionalist pressures are applied by those with political axes to grind.

It was a familiar story. The ripples of change moving out from the centres of quality became distorted with distance and repetition. A statement on mathematics by the well-known HMI, Edith Biggs, that she did not want children simply to learn tables by rote, but with understanding, became 'children should not learn their tables'. The idea that children should not be taught the mechanics of reading until they were intellectually ready was often interpreted as meaning that they should not be made ready. Similarly, the suggestion that children should learn science by carrying out their own practical enquiries all too readily became 'leave them alone with materials and they will teach themselves'.

Nevertheless, the wheel of change was gathering momentum and educational energy came from the example being set in the United States. The Russians had just (1957) put a man in space, and the US was determined to regain the initiative. Well-trained scientists and technologists were needed, and quickly. Millions of dollars became available, some of which were aimed at improving school science teaching. Then, someone had the bright idea of the curriculum development response.

The detailed response

The upheaval within the education profession, together with pressures from research, industry and the US example (Hoskins, 1965), stimulated several agencies to launch a series of initiatives:

• The British Association for the Advancement of Science/National Froebel Foundation (London) published *Children learning through scientific interests* (1966).
• The Ministry of Education/Oxford University Institute of Education published *An approach to primary science* (1969).
• The Nuffield Foundation set up its Junior Science Teaching Project (1964–1966), originally 7–13, later 5–13.

The approach of starting from an organised body of knowledge was, of course, diametrically opposed (though not necessarily less valid) to that of Nathan Isaacs (1958, 1963, 1965a & b, 1971), whose team had provided a range of practical experiences which prompted children to question, and so aroused interests which were channelled into scientific enquiries.

The Nuffield Project

The whole concept of the Nuffield Junior Science Project was remarkable and unprecedented in Britain. Never before had a centrally based team, employed by an organisation with no power or status within the educational establishment, produced materials to be tested by hundreds of teachers throughout the country. The project, recognising that the nature of the final examination largely determines the way teachers teach, successfully influenced the bodies responsible for setting external examinations. The result is that, 40 years on, while the original texts and guides may not be easily found in schools, attitudes towards science education and teaching have been profoundly influenced and changed.

The basic strategy

Materials were prepared by field-workers and then tested by teachers in pilot trial schools. Their findings were fed back to the central team who then rewrote the materials for publication. The Organiser and the team were given support and guidance by a Consultative Committee which included primary teachers, science specialists and HMI who kept the Secretary of State fully informed.

Although the Foundation had agreed to the project covering the age range 5–13, so as to include infant schools and give an overlap of two years with secondary schools, they drew the line at the inclusion of nursery schools and classes. This we believe to have been a sad decision, for in the world of nursery education was to be found much of the highest-quality and most forward-looking educational practice. Two so-called ESN (Educationally Sub-Normal) schools were included.

There was also a need for a series of workshop courses to prepare the teachers, and, in the case of this particular project, any Local Education Authority wishing to be included in the trials was asked to set up one or more teachers' centres.

Further training of teachers

From the earliest days it was appreciated that, if teachers were to be able to adopt the practices being advocated, they would have to be given a chance to learn through similar experiences at their own level. This, in turn, demanded a nation-wide series of in-service education workshops. Since British teachers were used to this kind of training, often on residential courses, there would be no problems in securing their release and support from normal duties. The only problem was who should provide them. In the end, the newly formed Schools Council took on the administrative responsibility, and the project, in collaboration with HMI and local education authorities, planned and staffed them.

Experience had shown that, if change were to be implemented, local education authority advisers and administrators would have to understand what the work was about, so they were invited to be members of each course. It was intended that the system would develop on the 'cascade' principle; following the national courses there would be similar ones organised by local education authority staff, and by team leaders in their areas. In this way, much valuable experience was accrued and fed back into the system. As the project developed, the nature of the courses became more closely related to the ways in which children learn science, with teachers being encouraged to investigate at their own level.

Implementation back at school remained a problem throughout the life of the project, indeed of all projects. This only began to be tackled effectively with the advent of large-scale support for advisory teachers in the mid 1980s (the ESG initiative – see Chapter 16).

Aims and objectives

A set of aims and objectives was never formalised and published as such, an omission which nowadays would be seen as unforgivable. But these were the earliest days of curriculum development with little or no experience on which to draw. All project workers, everywhere, were still gingerly feeling their way forward and building on experience. The evidence from projects which set out detailed objectives, especially when these were tied to assessment and testing (e.g. AAAS in the US) seemed to us to be putting project teams and teachers in a fairly rigid strait-jacket of subject matter and teaching methods. This was the last thing we wanted if we were to help free British primary education from its own traditional strait-jacket.

Even so, the team and the Consultative Committee all knew what the overall aims and objectives were, even though these were not written down. We ended up with a strongly Froebelian approach (see Chapter 2) but this was not deliberate. It simply grew out of the fact that we were constantly working with children and putting their educational needs at the top of the agenda. We all knew that we intended to help teachers to enable every child to learn as appropriately and effectively as possible (not just in science).

Some of the major objectives were dictated largely by the educational climate in which we found ourselves. Thus:
• *Our work must be based on what was known of children's intellectual development and learning processes. At the time, this meant taking account particularly of Piaget's work.*
• *Our work must constantly take account of what was seen as the best educational practice currently to be found in primary schools.*

The latter, however obvious and sensible it seemed, was to give us a great many problems, for while many teachers complained that the trial materials gave insufficient guidance, others argued that a more directed, less open-ended approach would be much less far along the road than they themselves had already gone. Indeed, teachers and advisers in Bristol, at a very early stage, made it clear that if we intended to produce practical kits, or work cards, they would refuse any invitation to join the project. There were equally strong feelings in some other authorities; for example, many infant and junior schools in Nottingham and the West Riding of Yorkshire expressed the same reservations.

With hindsight, this may be seen as a rather extreme viewpoint being put by a small, very advanced minority. But the project needed active support from people who could push and test the trial materials to their limits. We could not afford to alienate *any* local authority, let alone those in which much pioneering work had already taken place.
• *What we produced must take account of the various initiatives being taken by individuals and groups in different parts of the country.*

These included the Froebel and Ministry of Education projects already referred to, but also many teachers, college lecturers, LEA advisers, various authors of teachers' books, the newly founded (1963) Primary Science Sub-Committee of the ASE, and the devisers and producers of science programmes on radio and TV. Also from the USA came interesting materials, none more so than those of the Elementary Science Study (ESS) and other projects (see page 52).

• *All materials must be thoroughly tested by teachers in schools.*

Impact of the objectives on the nature of the project

The impact of setting the project in that particular context largely determined its nature. From then on, we moved steadily into an increasingly child-centred approach, a movement which gained momentum as children and then teachers in pre-pilot areas responded with increasing enthusiasm. It soon became apparent that, with readily available support from a team member, most teachers found the work exciting, manageable and rewarding. This was helped by the fact that our approach allowed work to develop not only at the pace of the children's capabilities, but also with the degree of flexibility that a teacher felt competent to control.

Given the right atmosphere, children *did* ask questions, *could* be trained to observe carefully, *could* design, perform and interpret experiments, and *could* predict. Many examples of this are given in the Nuffield Junior Science *Teacher's Guides* and one is quoted in the Plowden Report (CACE, 1967, para. 675). The following example also shows some of the capabilities that we began to see.

Thinking skills and problem solving

A first-year class in a grammar school in the North West was measuring the volume of a stone by displacing water in a measuring cylinder. They obviously found it very easy so I asked if they could possibly find the volume of a cube of sugar, using the same method.

They were, for a moment, non-plussed but soon the suggestions came: *'Wrap it in aluminium foil', 'Wrap it in clingfilm', 'Dip it in melted paraffin wax', 'Paint it with nail varnish'.*

After much thought, someone said, *'Don't use water – use a liquid that sugar won't dissolve in.'*

The following week I was with some 4th-year juniors in another school in the same city and I told them about finding the volume of a stone by displacement. They were not impressed because they had already done it.

So I asked them about the volume of a sugar lump and the ideas came rapidly: aluminium foil, clingfilm, paraffin wax, nail varnish, use a liquid other than water.

Finally a boy said, *'Put sugar in the water and stir it until no more will dissolve, then put the lump of sugar in.'*

I'm sad to say that I've never tried it but it would be a good idea to try some time.

As a consequence of what we saw, the team and the committee consciously took a decision not to produce a prescriptive written curriculum or syllabus, nor to produce work cards or kits. Instead, the effort would go into a series of teachers' guides, plus films, courses, and the establishment of teachers' centres.

A contributory factor, at once a benefit and a limitation, was the degree of autonomy enjoyed by individual schools and teachers. On the one hand, schools could feel free to experiment with new methods and ideas; on the other, the natural aversion that many people feel towards change meant that the project had to win teachers over and show that it could work. Happily, the team enjoyed working in classrooms and had a wealth of personal experience on which to draw. The project had to prove itself in an enormous variety of classroom scenarios, but it also had a rich range of professional environments in which to work.

Again with hindsight, it is easy to see the dilemma facing the team. At once, our objectives drove us relentlessly into an educationally 'pure' and uncompromising position, and made it difficult to produce materials giving adequate guidance to the many teachers who needed it.

The science

As the project proceeded, ideas crystallised on what science we should ask children to do. The evidence was that, given adequate team support, and hopefully even when that support was withdrawn, teachers could successfully manage classrooms so that children could learn science and, more importantly, learn *through* science.

Our overall 'philosophy' was now becoming clear:

In order to learn with understanding, human beings employ a series of learning strategies. One of these strategies is what we know as science, and we must help children to know when and how it is appropriate to use that strategy in the solution of a problem.

To achieve this aim, teachers were asked:
• to start work by observing the environment (outdoors or one constructed in the classroom);
• to help children observe, and order their observations, using all of their senses, within the limits of safety;
• to help children formulate questions based on their observations, and to recognise which kinds of questions might be answered through the processes of science (this meant that a questioning attitude had to be built into the daily life of the classroom);
• to help children suggest possible explanations for their observations (i.e. propose hypotheses);
• to help children devise ways of testing their hypotheses (i.e. design and carry out experiments, or other controlled enquiry);
• to help children examine and evaluate evidence;
• to help children, where appropriate, to predict and to test their predictions.
In other words, we committed ourselves to a process-based science education.

There were also a number of what might be called subordinate demands, although they were really no less important. For instance, we were very anxious to develop children's language skills through discussion, through reference books, through writing for, and talking to, a variety of audiences. We wanted them also to be able to use non-verbal communication skills such as painting, collage, model building, or movement. But overall, the important thing was for children to be able to decide which form of communication would be most appropriate.

Thus, the approach to science was based on practical exploration, was open-ended in nature, and was constantly interacting with all other aspects of the curriculum.

The underlying rationale

It is important that the reader should understand why the project placed such emphasis on children's own questions. It was a key aspect of the work and one which was later picked up by the 5/13 Nuffield/Schools Council Continuation Project.
We believed that:
• to learn effectively children need to ask appropriate questions and, if the learning is to be through science (even more so if they are to become professional scientists), they should learn what kinds of questions are answerable by science;
• children's own questions will almost certainly be, for them, the most relevant ones;
• if people (adults as well as children) ask their own questions, they are likely to pitch them at their own level of difficulty, as well as take into account what they, as individuals, already know and understand. That is, it seemed to us that no one can ask a completely pertinent question for anyone else. On the other hand, by asking their own questions, they are unlikely to be defeated by excessive difficulty; nor are they likely to find a too-easy question tedious.

This dedication to children's questions led us to another decision.

The decision not to produce work cards

Work cards were a popular aid to organising work. Indeed, teachers often made their own. Commercial products soon appeared, and these were a stage further away from the children and teachers for whom they had been originally written. Our reservations about the published work cards of the day were:
• They were often prescriptive, in many cases giving answers, and encouraging 'experiments to prove that something or other was true' rather than real enquiry.
• They depended not only on children being able to read, and to interpret, but also to follow and see the totality of a series of instructions, before they could even begin the practical work.
• Rarely, if ever, did they require children to use the processes of science, e.g. planning an experiment.
• Never did they allow children to ask their own questions.
Similar reservations could be, and were, levelled at commercially produced kits.

In the view of the project, its open-ended, child-centred approach would allow children to proceed at their own natural pace, following enquiries of their own devising, and so would have maximum motivating effect. It also reduced the element of competition with peers, which many children found irksome, even depressing, after continual comparative failure. It was intended that children should compete with themselves, and even work together co-operatively to raise their own standards of performance. This did, indeed, happen.

A degree of flexibility for the teacher

This was another advantage of the system being advocated, for there is no doubt that many teachers, then as now, had difficulty in organising practical work in an overcrowded, poorly equipped classroom.

Experience soon showed that team members were able to give valuable help and support. Once teachers had overcome the difficulties involved, they usually said that individual and small-group work not only enabled children to learn more effectively, but that they themselves could exercise greater control over the situation. It was important, of course, to reassure teachers that very few of them would be able to start with a complete class breakdown into small groups (a limitation applying to children as well as teachers); indeed some of them might never go beyond the stage of standing in front of the whole class and allowing individual children to do some practical task for all to see.

It was always intended that the degree of flexibility should be high so as to accommodate every variation in teaching ability, experience and personal teaching preference. In any case, it was important to realise that from time to time a teacher would need to bring a whole class together, possibly to survey the present state of the class's work, to teach a specific technique that might be causing problems, or even to feed in new information so as to maintain the impetus of the enquiry.

How scientific enquiry was introduced

The ways in which scientific enquiry was introduced also reflected this flexibility of approach. For example:
• it might be a straightforward piece of science in its own right as decreed by the timetable;
• it might arise out of the teaching of some other subject on the timetable;
• it might be a carefully constructed aspect of a general topic, e.g. energy or homes;
• it might (the most difficult of all for most teachers) arise out of some casual incident or comment, such as a 9-year-old boy announcing that men were digging a hole in the road outside the school.

Contrary to what was sometimes suggested, this practical approach did not reduce the need for books but encouraged their use. Children wanted to read about the science they had been investigating. Books were used for reference purposes, for checking findings against received wisdom which, in turn, could force a critical examination of their own experimenting. In such a scenario, it goes without saying that film, slides, radio and TV were all essential aids, extensions, or stimulators of investigation (Nuffield Junior Science *Teacher's Guide 1*, pp. 217–260).

Finally, we were anxious that teachers should be aware that many famous discoveries could be imitated, for instance Galileo's supposed timing of the chandelier in the Cathedral at Pisa (many a child – and teacher – has been surprised by the near impossibility of counting a pulse in the wrist while trying to count the swings of a pendulum ...).

This aspect of science was set out in a small teachers' booklet, *Science and history*, which also reinforced the fact that some great investigations (Walter Reed's awesome experiments with yellow fever on human volunteers) cannot be repeated for obvious reasons. But they make incredibly exciting accounts of scientific enquiry when read or told by the teacher.

Flexibility there certainly was, although some of the approaches suggested proved too difficult for all but the exceptional teachers.

One of the Nuffield Junior Science teacher's background booklets

Nuffield Junior Science

Teacher's Background Booklet **Science and History**

Collins

Subject matter

Once the decision was made to place emphasis on 'processes', the limited timescale, the small size of the team, and the situation in the schools determined the direction in which the project would go from then on. For example:

• The decision meant that the vast majority of effort went into developing a process approach.

• Only a tiny proportion of teachers had received any training whatsoever in the use of processes. They did not know how to ask or recognise an appropriate question, or a hypothesis. They did not know what was meant by a variable, let alone how to control one. They could not design experiments, and they had no experience of evaluating evidence and drawing valid conclusions.

• Most teachers had only very limited scientific knowledge on which to draw and, even then, much of it made little sense to them.

The result was that we had to say 'At present we must concern ourselves more with how children learn than with what they learn', even though this was often interpreted as 'it doesn't matter if they don't learn anything'.

Nevertheless, the problem of subject matter was a difficult one and one which was never solved. Probably, we did not give it the attention it warranted from the start, although all the project team would argue that we had established the right priorities by concentrating on process.

Once they had begun to master the art of initiating scientific enquiry, teachers often found that they had difficulty in sustaining and developing it, and a knowledge of subject matter was a prime factor in finding a solution to this problem.

Heads and teachers were also worried about the perennial problem of repetition of work in successive years, and of isolating scientific problems within topic work or environmental studies. The importance of this was emphasised by Nathan Isaacs when he spoke to the team about the young child's view of the world. He said, '*Yes, it is true that a young child sees the world as a whole thing and does not see it in terms of adult conceived disciplines, but it is important that the teacher should recognise when a child is doing science, or mathematics, or history, and that the teacher should know what is meant by "good science, good mathematics and good history".*' Understanding of both processes and subject matter would certainly be essential if teachers were to achieve that difficult target. Of course, the problem was not simply related to science, but could be applied to the whole curriculum.

As has already been explained, a strategy for dissemination and teacher development was the publication of teachers' guides with some films and information booklets. The major strategy for teacher support was the development of teachers' centres and in this we had the backing of a very influential HMI, Edith Biggs.

Teachers' centres

Prior to the project, only a few local authorities had teachers' centres (e.g. Birmingham and Carlisle), but across the country there was an enthusiastic response to the project's decision to expand the network.

The country-wide scale of the undertaking and the quality and extent of the resourcing was new. Most local education authorities set up well-furnished, comfortable premises and appointed a centre leader to conduct the day-to-day running. There was no precedent for work in teachers' centres, but we were clear that they should reflect local needs and opinions. Essentially, they were to be for teachers and, as far as possible, to be administered by teachers. They were to be places where teachers could meet to discuss the work they were doing for the project, where they could explore books and practical investigations. They were also places where courses could be run.

All centres took on their own special characteristics, usually reflecting the character and enthusiasms of the leader and the LEA. Sometimes teachers themselves took on the government and policy making. However, the significant aspect of teachers' centres was that curriculum development was moved closer to where it should be based – on the classroom floor. There had been an injection of money, enthusiasm, and impetus in a centrally based organisation which now found itself operating through teams in the field and through locally based centres. In time, they became not only places where training took place, but also the points of origin of new curricular materials devised by local teachers.

In time, in a very few cases, the generation of new curricular ideas moved even nearer to the grassroots, into individual schools or groups of schools.

A remarkable effect of the project's acting within teachers' centres was a fundamental change in teacher attitudes to what they were prepared to share professionally. Traditionally, entry into classrooms was resented, even feared and seen as unprofessional. For instance, I once admired some science work in a classroom and asked the (experienced) teacher if she had shown it to Mrs X whose class was doing similar things. She said, '*What, and have her pinch all my ideas?*'

However, when centrally produced materials were being tested, it was essential that failure as well as success should be discussed and recorded. This was a breakthrough. Until then, most talked little about what went on in their classrooms apart from anecdotal chitchat, or displaying the best for parents and colleagues. Now, they began to talk about difficulties and problems – many of which were common, or at least widespread – and to share ideas instead of guarding them jealously. Teaching was becoming teamwork.

When we first insisted on teachers' centres, we had no idea of the importance they would take on, but even by the end of the project's life, the national picture was gratifying. By the early 70s, there were over 700 centres, activity was at a high level, and there was even a national association of centre leaders. Not only were teachers sharing ideas but courses built *classroom visits* into their plans!

By the late 80s, severe financial cuts had caused the closure of many centres, with many of those remaining struggling to pay their way in the market economy. Hopefully, if the financial situation improves, centres will again be recognised as valuable assets. If not, it is vital to discover and develop an effective way of allowing teachers to work together and share expertise. There are real tensions in the market place but the cost of not valuing and using co-operative activities of enthusiastic teachers must not be underestimated.

Links and liaisons overseas

The Nuffield Junior Science Project had important links and influences overseas too. Visits and invitations were made and offered by Professor David Hawkins, Director of the Elementary Science Study (ESS) in Watertown, USA, and Norman Massey of the Ontario Education Department, both of whom modified their ideas and publications in the light of the successful work of the project.

One of the results of this successful liaison was an extended study by Paul Park (Ontario/Ford Foundation Grant) who acknowledged the importance of Nuffield in his own project and booklet, *The world of the child*:

What we saw in visit after visit [to schools] were children pursuing interests at their own rate on questions of their own design ... Basic to the Nuffield philosophy is the assumption that children learn through the solution of practical problems that have significance for them. The Early School Environmental Study [the Canadian Project] accepts this practical problem-solving approach and has expanded it beyond the science framework into the learning of language, mathematics and social studies.

Yet another result of this liaison was a development of the link with the ESS project under Dave Hawkins. The funding agency, Educational Services Incorporated, funded a member of the Nuffield team, Bob Carlisle (now in the Education Department of the University of British Columbia in Vancouver), to travel to Africa and run an elementary science programme in a number of countries.

Another link was with Lillian Weber who was based in City College, New York, and ran an *'open classroom project for teachers in Harlem and the Bronx'*. This project had fought a tremendous battle with authorities for survival and funding and had to prove itself in terms of performance on New York City Standard Tests. These tests were loaded with white middle-class language and thinking, set in classrooms where sloping desks were screwed to the floor and children were forbidden to work in corridors. Screens were erected to separate project classes and ordinary classes so that the latter would not be contaminated. Nevertheless, Lillian Weber's work began to influence thinking in NY education. She acknowledged the effect of Nuffield Science on her thinking in her book, *The English infant school and informal education* (New York: Prentice Hall) when she wrote: *'For Ron [Wastnedge] – this book is part yours. Without my contact with Nuffield Junior Science it would have been different and incomplete.'*

The second phase of the project

The overall strategy of the Nuffield projects was that, year by year, more authorities and schools would be introduced, and this was true of the Junior Science project. In September 1965 a further 40 education authorities were included, and in September 1966 the net was thrown completely open.

The peculiar timing of the project (starting January 1964 and ending December 1966) led, understandably, to problems and dissatisfaction on the part of the authorities who came in at the end and who felt they had been treated somewhat unfairly. The situation was further exacerbated by the fact that all the employers who had generously seconded team members expected them to be back in post by September 1966, leaving only the Organiser to run down the project as smoothly and gently as possible.

Furthermore, not everyone was convinced that the approach would work. When the books were launched in 1967, we had 10 children with their teacher from Primrose Hill Primary School in London actually working so that journalists and politicians could see the approach in action. Sir Ronald Gould (General Secretary, NUT) said he thought it was great but that teachers would never manage it, since it was too difficult.

The way ahead

As the end of the project approached it was absolutely clear that much work remained to be done. The Nuffield Foundation felt that it had made its financial contribution and was not able to continue funding an extended project.

The Organiser then decided to do two things. First, he asked the Foundation to employ him for three days a week for a term so that he could maintain contact with second-phase areas from home. Secondly, he spoke to the Schools Council steering committee and tried to persuade them to fund a continuation project. The outcome was that the Nuffield Foundation and Schools Council jointly funded 'The Nuffield/ Schools Council Continuation Project'. Its Director was retired HMI Len Ennever and the project eventually became the Schools Council 5/13 Project.

Seeing things from the child's point of view

Thinking things through

A 6-year-old was explaining to the inspector what she had done in her study of growing seeds. She displayed impressive knowledge of the effects of giving water to the seeds and of not giving water. In order to test whether or not the young investigator had a measure of deeper understanding, the inspector asked, *'What do you think would happen to the seeds if you gave them lemonade instead of water?'* After a few moments of thought, the pupil replied, *'I think they would still grow, but they would come up frizzy.'*

Brilliant! This indicates a very high order of thinking: explaining, or offering a hypothesis. Her response also indicates knowledge of materials and their properties – the little girl knew of the similarity of water and lemonade and therefore expected a similar outcome, namely, growth. However, she also knew of the dissimilarity between water and lemonade (frizzy) and predicted a corresponding outcome (frizzy plants).

The difficulties of accurate observation

A 9-year-old had been studying worms and their key role in moving and aerating soil. This was done by observing changes in the school's wormery. The boy had been given good guidance in the features of science investigation, including that of providing accurate descriptions, in words, numbers and pictures, of what was observed. The inspector, on reading the boy's account, was both elated and anxious. He read, *'My worm wriggles a lot so I can't be sure of its length. I tried measuring it and I reckon it is 20 cm – at a stretch.'*

The inspector could not determine whether or not the pupil's diagram of the worm's 'face' showed anxiety.

What does one say?

There was a science problem in the nursery class of the infants school. John had asked a hard question and none of the teachers felt secure in offering a suitable response. *'Well,'* said the Head, *'we'll leave it until Thursday when the inspector is due to call. He should know.'*

Thursday came and, as arranged, the inspector arrived. After the customary pleasantries, the Head said, *'We are very glad you've come, because the children have been asking us hard science questions all week. Anyway, we told them to keep their questions until Thursday when you would answer them.'* The inspector felt a deep sense of foreboding, partly because of this further manifestation of the commonly-held view that to every science question there is a 'right' answer.

They removed to the nursery class and John was invited to demonstrate his problem to the inspector. It was this. When he brought his two little plastic cars, one in each hand, close together, bonnet to bonnet, they jumped together. On separating them and bringing them together again, but this time the bonnet of one to the boot of the other, they would not go together, no matter how hard he tried. The delight on his face was a sight to behold. *'Howzat, mister?'*

The behaviour of John's cars would be described by scientists, when speaking to each other, by reference to theories of magnetism, with accompanying specific terminology and mathematics. But such an 'explanation', although 'right' for the scientists, would be wholly 'wrong' for John, so his particular question would remain unanswered (or responded to).

One of his teachers, drawing on her long experience of young children, offered the comment, *'Very young children see everything in personal terms, so perhaps when the cars cling together we could say that "they like each other". When they refuse (?) to go together, "they don't like each other".'*

Yes, that seems reasonable for John and he is the one that matters, since he asked the question. But will John's brother, who is 10, be content or will John himself when he reaches the age of 10? Probably not. So what is the response to *'Howzat, mister?'*

Ron Wastnedge

References

Central Advisory Council for Education (1967) *Children and their primary schools* (The Plowden Report). London: HMSO.

Hoskins, D. (1965) Report to ESS on visit to Nuffield Junior Science Program. In *Archives, Nathan Isaacs Collection*, File ref. NI/C/21. Institute of Education, University of London.

Isaacs, N. (1958) *Early scientific trends in children*. London: National Froebel Foundation.

Isaacs, N. (1963) Children's scientific interests. In *First years in school*. Studies in Education. London: Institute of Education, University of London.

Isaacs, N. (1965a) Memorandum for the Plowden Committee. *Froebel Journal*, 2. London.

Isaacs, N. (1965b) *Piaget – Some answers to teachers' questions*. London: National Froebel Foundation.

Isaacs, N. (1971) *A brief introduction to Piaget*. New York: Agatha Press.

National Froebel Foundation (1966) *Children learning through scientific interests*. London.

Nuffield Science Teaching Project (1967). London: Collins

Teacher's Guide 1 (ed. Wastnedge, E. R.)

Teacher's Guide 2 (ed. Wastnedge, E. R.)

Apparatus: a source book of information and ideas

Animals and plants: a source book of information and ideas

Teacher's Background Booklets:

Science and history

Autumn into winter

Mammals in classrooms

The imperfections of assessing children on the basis of the 3 'R's

Class 9 (10-year-olds) had been studying various types of travel and transport, in the course of which they had read about rockets and made models of rockets. From their reading, they had learned about the high speeds of rockets and gone on to learn that the fastest speed of all is that of light.

The inspector noticed that one boy was working on his own, doing some language work. The class teacher explained, *'He's having a little difficulty with reading and writing so he's doing some extra work, but he's very interesting to talk to.'* With this half-implied suggestion as encouragement, the inspector went to speak with the boy and soon appreciated the teacher's comment. After some minutes of conversation about the rocket project, the boy offered his book to the inspector. What a surprise, not to say a touch of disappointment. The writing was unreadable; it seemed to be based on an unfamiliar alphabet, not to say a foreign orthography

Keen not to embarrass the boy, the inspector explained that he would collect the books of other pupils and go to a quiet corner. With this degree of subterfuge hopefully accomplishing its desired purpose, the inspector sought the help of the class teacher who, of course, could read the boy's work. She read, *'The speed of light is the biggest of all. If I could travel with the speed of light I would leave my shadow behind.'* The inspector noted that all the other pupils simply reported that the speed of light was 186,000 miles per second.

Note: It is often the case that the most lateral thinkers are slow at developing their reading and writing skills.

'Knowing' is more than 'knowing about'

The inspector visited a very small primary school serving a Welsh rural community. A recent attack of foot and mouth disease had decimated the stock of local farms and caused considerable distress to the pupils because of the inevitable slaughter of 'close friends'. By way of therapy as much as anything else, the pupils were encouraged to write about 'The foot and mouth disease at our farm'.

One pupil wrote at length, but it was not this feature that caught the inspector's eye or engaged his interest. The first page was exemplary in all the requirements of language composition: neat handwriting, pertinent use of paragraphs, correct punctuation. The substance of this page was mostly factual and indicated a detached attitude. At the start of the second page the mood changed. It was about Daisy the cow being dragged dead across the farmyard. Thereafter all conventions and composition were abandoned and the words were blurred under tear stains.

Neville Evans

From *Humour, muse, enterprise* (1998) published by The Leonard Cheshire Homes and Ty Hafan, The Children's Hospice in Wales.

Celebrating A Century of Primary Science

ERRATA

The Publishers wish to draw your attention to two errors of fact on page 56:

The correct title of the book mentioned should be *Humor Muse Inspiration* (1998)

The book was written *in support of* The Leonard Cheshire Homes and Ty Hafan, The Children's Hospice in Wales, not published by the Aforementioned.

ASE apoligises for any inconvenience these errors may cause.

7 Changing perspectives

Helen Rapson

ASE Primary Science and the Learning Through Science Project

Helen Rapson graduated in agricultural botany and then worked in a commercial plant nursery before doing a PhD in plant pathology at Imperial College, London. Her marriage to a civil engineer took her around the world and she taught science in European and Asian secondary schools. On her return to the UK, she worked for many years in colleges of education, teaching science to trainee teachers. She was the founder editor of *ASE Primary Science*. Helen has always been committed to developing opportunities for children with special educational needs. After the Warnock Report (1978) she worked with Doug Kincaid and Roy Richards in the Learning Through Science Project to research and write materials for children with special educational needs and their teachers.

My own learning about primary science

In 1967, I was living in Wisbech, Cambridgeshire, teaching various aspects of biology at the Ely College. From 1961 to 1963 I had taught in secondary schools in Nairobi and was now looking for work in London so I could rejoin my husband who had recently been sent there.

This was a time of expansion in teacher training and the colleges of education were recruiting tutors who, academically, were sufficiently well qualified to be acceptable to universities, now saddled with the new BEd degrees. My first application was to the Primary Annexe of Battersea College of Education. My lack of training as a primary teacher and complete ignorance of all aspects of the development of young children were obviously not taken into consideration at interview. Swiftly I found I had a job – in a beautiful old house set in lovely surroundings, with pleasant and welcoming colleagues, near to my home. But I knew little about a large part of the work involved!

In retrospect I realise how fortunate I was to work at Battersea, which had a primary course with an unusually high professional content, and to be joining a Head of Science who was to be influential in primary science throughout the country for years to come – Roy Richards. With his light-handed and light-hearted initiation into primary science, my education in college began, with generous help from tutors in literacy and mathematics and all other aspects of primary professional work. Above all, I valued those members of the education staff who believed that encouraging all aspects of the development of children was the business of the good teacher, and that the best way of achieving that was through integrated work adapted to meet the needs of individual children.

A charismatic, tall, thin, much-wrinkled ex-East End headteacher, Charles Zoeftig, was deputed to take me on many teaching-practice visits. This was an almost magical experience: he was loved by all, and his discussions with students and the help he gave them illuminated the theory I was absorbing.

At the end of my first year Roy Richards dropped a bombshell: he had been seconded for a year to the Schools Council Science 5/13 Project, and I was to be left with both the professional and main subject work – a stimulating and exciting variety! In the event, Roy did not return but resigned when his first year with Science 5/13 led to a post for the life of the project.

At Battersea, the professional primary science course, about 37 hours in college, was a compulsory part of the training and practice of all primary students. It was moved from the first year into the second; by then the students were ready to tackle what they perceived to be a difficult component of the curriculum, and the change was a complete success. The transition year gave me time to follow some of the other student professional courses and, most importantly, to do some teaching myself in infant and junior schools.

In 1981 I retired. By then, Battersea was a part of the Polytechnic of the South Bank and included a nursery section. Over the years, I had come to understand much more about primary-aged children and the ways they could, and should, be taught. I still firmly believe that an integrated subject approach, taking into account the development and aptitude of each individual child, is the one which brings most success and teacher satisfaction, although undoubtedly it is much harder to prepare and to organise than is generally appreciated. It also demands a high degree of mutual respect and co-operation between teacher and children.

My daughter, a trained and experienced secondary science teacher, has for the past two years, for family reasons, been dividing her time between acting as a teacher's assistant in a reception class and supply-teaching in the same primary school. I was interested a few weeks ago to hear her say with amazement:

The only teachers in our school who really have time to do a first-class job are those who have no other commitments, are single and have no children. All the others are under pressure all the time!

ASE Primary Science

Early in the summer of 1979, Brian Atwood, the then General Secretary of the ASE, asked if I would be willing to edit a 'science newsletter' for primary school teachers. Seven or eight people, most of them practising primary teachers, had agreed to help. They eventually became the first Advisory Editorial Board, a committee which was of very considerable help to me, particularly in scrutinising the drafts of the 30 issues which I edited.

ASE was mainly concerned with secondary education, although intermittently since 1963 it had had a Primary Sub-Committee which worked hard to spread some understanding of what primary science could and should be. The sub-committee had also written some excellent primary publications, some of which are still, in the year 2000, widely bought and used. But the vast majority of the membership thought of primary science as a simple, first-stage version of secondary work. There was no primary membership, and, apart from the members of the Primary Sub-Committee, few people associated with the organisation had the faintest idea of the philosophy of primary education or of the development (social, intellectual, physical and emotional) of young children. All this, of course, was the business of the primary school teacher.

Since 1964, there had been three important national projects concerned with teaching science in the primary school and a fourth was under way. Early in 1978, the Secretary of State for Education, Shirley Williams, had asked the Association to consider ways in which science teaching for all ages and abilities might be improved, and ASE felt the time was right to produce something – a publication? – that would help primary teachers. Most of these teachers were very hesitant, having little personal scientific knowledge and believing it too specialised and difficult an area to tackle. They often failed to see the opportunities for scientific investigation that were constantly before them; nor did they realise that already they frequently used the methods of science.

ASE and the Advisory Editorial Board gradually felt their way towards the type of publication and the organisation of its distribution that might be successful and helpful – and affordable. Deliberately, we teachers kept the paper short – 'to be read within a coffee break' – just four A4 sides per issue, one issue per term. Local education authorities were invited to buy it in bulk, and to distribute it with their own primary schools' mail. A trial edition was circulated for comment and orders in the autumn of 1979; it received approval and went into production in the spring of 1980.

Audrey Randall, a Board member who was the Head of a Hertfordshire Infant School, offered the first material. After an enjoyable afternoon, I left her school laden with enormous brightly coloured drawings, paintings, charts and children's writing, few less than 50 x 50 cm and many much larger, wondering what on earth to do with it all. Only four A4 sides? I discovered how selectively to cut, enlarge, reduce and rearrange children's work so that it told a whole story in very little space; occasionally I had to put their words into typescript. Little other explanation was needed, and that first work, with a short editorial describing how it fulfilled the processes of science – observing and questioning, experimenting and measuring, concluding and communicating – made the trial and first issue of *ASE Primary Science*.

Always we published work done by practising primary teachers, in ordinary classrooms. We hoped that it demonstrated the science in everyday primary school activities, and that it introduced new ideas and ways of working and thus encouraged other teachers to follow up things they and their own pupils found interesting. The paper became popular with teachers, and grew to have a print run of over 30,000 copies.

Finding material was always the biggest problem. Few teachers were confident enough to send us their work: I had to go out and find it. Science advisers and advisory teachers suggested schools to visit, and sometimes I had news of science exhibitions and science fairs, and friends and colleagues helped as did the Advisory Editorial Board. It became even more difficult as the pressures on primary teachers increased. Sadly too, in later years they were so anxious about fulfilling all the objectives they were set that they had not the time, the energy or the confidence to continue to help children to explore topics from the viewpoint of all relevant disciplines. Children's literacy skills were rarely practised in describing real observations, or in explaining how they themselves had investigated a problem. Nor were mathematical skills developed in choosing and using appropriate ways of measuring and recording real data – nor children's ability to reason by asking, *What have we found out?'* and so on.

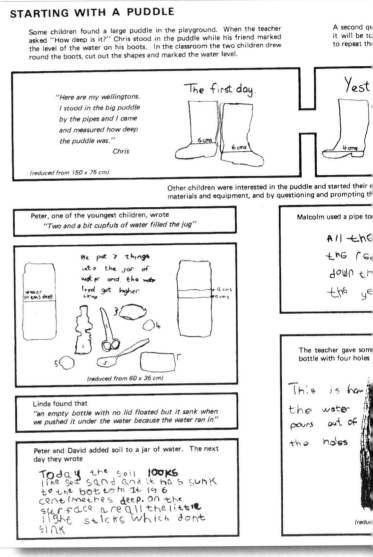

STARTING WITH A PUDDLE

Some children found a large puddle in the playground. When the teacher asked "How deep is it?" Chris stood in the puddle while his friend marked the level of the water on his boots. In the classroom the two children drew round the boots, cut out the shapes and marked the water level.

The first day.

"Here are my wellingtons.
I stood in the big puddle
by the pipes and I came
and measured how deep
the puddle was."
Chris

6 cms   6 cms

(reduced from 150 x 75 cm)

Other children were interested in the puddle and started their [...] materials and equipment, and by questioning and prompting th[...]

Peter, one of the youngest children, wrote
"Two and a bit cupfuls of water filled the jug"

We put 7 things into the jar of water and the water level got higher

water 10 cms deep.

(reduced from 60 x 35 cm)

Linda found that
"an empty bottle with no lid floated but it sank when we pushed it under the water because the water ran in"

Peter and David added soil to a jar of water. The next day they wrote

Today the soil looks like wet sand and it has sunk to the bottom It is 6 centimetres deep. on the surface are all the little light sticks which dont sink

Malcolm used a pipe to[...]

The teacher gave som[...] bottle with four holes

This is how the water pours out of the holes

However, writing 10 years later, I do feel rather more optimistic. Surely the pendulum should swing again towards more freedom for primary teachers so that they are allowed to teach in the way they personally do best, so that the methods of primary science again become a valued learning tool.

At the end of 1989 I retired as Editor, after ten happy and interesting years. I was delighted that Audrey Randall, a stalwart and active supporter of the paper since it started, was to be the new Editor.

The centre spread from issue number 1 of *ASE Primary Science* published in spring 1980, showing work done in Brookland County Infants' School, Hertfordshire

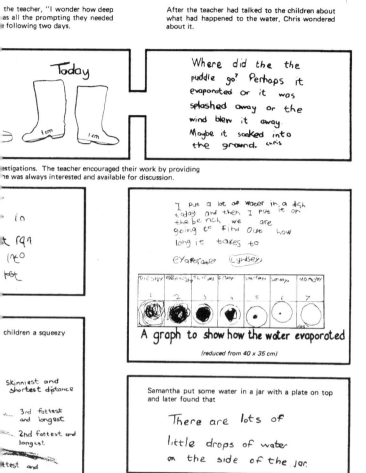

the teacher, "I wonder how deep
as all the prompting they needed
e following two days.

After the teacher had talked to the children about what had happened to the water, Chris wondered about it.

Today

Where did the the puddle go? Perhaps it evaporated or it was splashed away or the wind blew it away. Maybe it soaked into the ground. *chris*

estigations. The teacher encouraged their work by providing
e was always interested and available for discussion.

I put a lot of water in a dish today and then I put it on the bench we are going to find out how long it takes to evaporate. (Lyndsey)

A graph to show how the water evaporated

(reduced from 40 x 35 cm)

children a squeezy

Skinniest and shortest distance

3rd fattest and longest

2nd fattest and longest

ttest and longest distance

m)

Samantha put some water in a jar with a plate on top and later found that

There are lots of little drops of water on the side of the jar.

The teacher thought that each experiment was valuable in itself: if one led to another, as in the column above, it was because the children thought of it for themselves, perhaps after talking to her.

Science for children with learning difficulties

In 1978, the Warnock Committee recommended that the term 'children with learning difficulties' should be used for any who have special educational needs and that, in the almost complete absence of appropriate teaching materials and help for their teachers, attention should be given to curriculum development for these children. Accordingly, in 1979, the Learning Through Science Project, sponsored by the Schools Council and the Scottish Education Department, was extended by a full-time, two-year appointment to start to meet this need. Doug Kincaid and I shared it, each of us working half time, and Roy Richards, the project director, also made a substantial contribution.

Although most of these children were in ordinary schools, it appeared that science was hardly ever taught to them. Yet the more we looked into it, the more obvious it was that scientific work of the kind done in primary schools would fulfil many of their educational needs. But all too often, either because they were disruptive or because they were sent away to do remedial work, children with learning difficulties were excluded from all the exciting practical activities that would have aroused their curiosity and encouraged all aspects of their development.

Above all, as a precursor of all future educational progress, they needed to succeed – and a simple practical investigation to answer a question will yield a result. It was something that all these children could do to some extent, depending on the nature of their disability.

Their teacher would have a vital role to play, as the person who helped children to raise questions and encouraged the children's interests, helped them to plan investigations and record results, and talked to them afterwards about their findings. Admittedly there would be problems. Steps would have to be small, and often reinforced in an interesting way; special methods needed to be devised to allow non-literate children to measure and record their work. We aimed to help teachers to do these things. Eventually, we devised ten units, some quite new and others adapted from topics that most children enjoy. With thought for the busy teacher, our ideas were explained as graphically as possible.

Trials took place in at least six schools in each of six LEAs; my own visits ranged from the industrial West Riding to rural Avon. In each school, several classes were involved. There were some surprising successes, such as the 9-year-old boy who began to read simple text practically overnight because he was so excited by his experiments with batteries and bulbs and desperately wanted to find out more. And there were some excited children, such as those who offered to make me a cup of tea *'the proper way, Miss'*, and explained *'We found out that you* must *warm the pot, 'specially if it's a thick one, or else the tea isn't really hot.'* Much more often progress was slow but discernible; the children enjoyed their work and their attitude to it, and to each other, changed. Amongst other things they became noticeably more responsible.

No teacher found it easy to organise, but often it was tackled with a whole mixed-ability class or group; sometimes with the less-able children working with the more-able; sometimes, and much more successfully, with the less-able working together in small groups. The work itself was not special to children with learning difficulties, just specially presented to help their teachers to offer science to such children.

Two years sped by all too fast, from initial discussions with teachers, to devising the work, visiting schools which were trialling the materials, and final revision and preparation for publication of a book for teachers. We seemed just to be getting into our stride when we had to stop. But enough had been done for our purpose: some of the material of the main project had been modified and new material had been written – enough to help teachers get started. We hoped the interest and excitement of the work, and the progress it helped children with learning difficulties to achieve in social, physical and intellectual skills, would provide sufficient impetus to take it forward.

Do you take tea?

Trying out the workpack on 'Materials' for the Learning Through Science Project took my colleague Doug Kincaid to a school where the children were testing teapots to find which kind of teapot keeps tea hot longest.

At the end of the day, the teacher found two girls outside the lavatories with one of them in tears. Apparently, among the teapots they had mustered for testing was one used by the staff. In emptying it, the teapot lid had gone down the toilet pan.

'Never mind', said the teacher. 'Dry your eyes! It's not the end of the world.'

'But we've always got it back before', said the wet-eyed girl.

Roy Richards

8 First and second generation primary science projects ∞

Wynne Harlen

Laying the foundations in the 1960s and 1970s: Science 5/13

Wynne Harlen, OBE, currently edits *Primary Science Review*. Since leaving the post of Director of the Scottish Council for Research in Education in 1999, she had been Visiting Professor at the University of Bristol and undertakes various consultancies in primary science in the UK and abroad. In the past, Wynne has been Professor of Science Education at the University of Liverpool and was a member of the Secretary of State's initial working group on the National Curriculum for Science. She has directed several research and development projects and is the author of a number of books and articles on primary science.

In 1966, I was working as a research fellow at the Institute of Education (as it then was) of Bristol University on the evaluation of a curriculum development project known as the Oxford Primary Science Project (1963–67). I studied four groups of schools – two involved in the Oxford project in different parts of the country and two groups of 'control' schools. One group of controls had no science and the other was of schools involved in the Nuffield Junior Science (NJS) Project, then in its final year. The Oxford and the Nuffield were 'first generation' primary science projects, being part of the wave of science projects begun in response to the concern about the state of science education that was widespread in the UK as in many other countries in the 60s.

I will not bore you with the details of the early work on which I cut my teeth in evaluation and in assessment in primary science. The only reason for mentioning it is to set the scene for my involvement in Science 5/13, which started in Bristol in 1967, funded by the Nuffield Foundation, the Schools Council and, later, by the Scottish Education Department. I was in the right place at the right time and was appointed evaluator of this new project, where I stayed until 1973 when I moved to Reading University to direct my own project, Progress in Learning Science. At first I was part-time (my daughter was born in 1967) but later became full-time. The project continued until 1975, led by Len Ennever, previously an HMI. The core team comprised Sheila Parker (later Sheila Jelly), Don Radford, Albert James, Roy Richards and Anne Mattock, as secretary.

Science 5/13 was originally conceived as a continuation of the NJS project but, as a second generation project, it soon developed its own approach. It departed in two particular respects from its predecessor. One of these was to state objectives for children learning science. There had been some resistance to this by the NJS team, who had made only very general statements about what children might achieve through science activities, on the grounds that not enough was known about this and that to state objectives might needlessly limit children's horizons (a far cry from attainment targets!).

The second point concerned the type of material being produced by the project. The development of units for teachers on specific topics was intended to give teachers more specific ideas for children's activities than the general guidelines and examples of the NJS materials. The units were developed in close collaboration with teachers, the project staff frequently visiting classrooms, sometimes working directly with children and often meeting with teachers at centres to discuss and display children's work. The concept of a unit was gradually refined in this way and, when complete drafts were prepared, they were given year-long trials, before revision and publication.

Time for thinking: where is it now?

This may seem a somewhat leisurely time-scale: an eight-year project; four years before the first units were published; a full year for trialling draft materials. Moreover, each summer a week-long course was organised for teachers and administrators, or for college lecturers. These courses, held in various parts of the country, always included a weekend, with activities only on Saturday mornings and so plenty of time for informal discussion, networking and reflection – also for drinking the excellent sherry that Len Ennever always laid on in small barrels from Harvey's of Bristol! Of course, to those of us involved it seemed not at all leisurely. We had to share our ideas with people who had little notion of what we now recognise as primary science; we had to convince some who were sceptical; we provided hands-on experience to convey what was intended and opportunities for feedback on the units and the evaluation procedures. But we had the time to do these things.

The team also had time, especially in the first four years of the project, to try out different approaches to helping teachers and to gather evidence to decide which to pursue and which to abandon. What was produced, as a result, was truly innovative and the Science 5/13 units were leaders in the field for several years. They did not suit every teacher, for change in practice requires far more than the adoption of a particular scheme, but they provided a goal and a vision of what was possible. Not many subsequent projects have had the luxury of time to think and try things out as the Science 5/13 team did. Time is always pressing and corners consequently are cut. Significantly, I think the next big breakthrough in primary science materials came 20 years after the start of Science 5/13, with the next Nuffield-funded project, Nuffield Primary Science, which was based on research carried out over four years and lasted in total for six years (1987–1993). In haste we make progress slowly!

Trials and tribulations in the Science 5/13 Project

My role in the Science 5/13 Project was to clarify the objectives and evaluate trials of the draft units. To this end, for the first set of trials, I devised 'tests' for children, classroom observation schedules and many different kinds of questionnaires for teachers' feedback. The test material was by no means conventional. We wanted to present children with real situations and questions which would probe whether or not they had developed the idea or the process skill needed to answer successfully. However, to do this would have required individual administration, which was impractical with the numbers involved. The most attractive alternative, to avoid too much dependence on verbal ability and other disadvantages of paper-and-pencil tests, was to use moving film. The type chosen was 8 mm film that could be put into film loops for use in a projector with an integral rear-projection screen and suitable for use in daylight.

So sequences were filmed both indoors and outdoors, showing situations or events chosen to present problems relevant to the topic of each unit. There was also a more general set of questions relating to process skills objectives and to children's liking for various activities. In operation, a whole class could be tested at once. After the children had watched a segment of film, the film was stopped while the administrator posed a question and the children recorded their answers in booklets by ticking one of the alternative responses which were also read out. The tests were given to both trial and control classes and as pre-trial and post-trial measures.

As I recorded in the account of the evaluation of Science 5/13, the making, editing, repairing and remaking of the film loops was arduous and time-consuming. Apart from trying to develop 8 mm filming skills (which I haven't used since), devising the test items brought about detailed probing of the learning outcomes intended and so had a beneficial backwash on the thinking that went into each unit.

The filming was fun too. I can't help repeating this story:

One team member, Sheila Parker (later Sheila Jelly), helped to produce the films by manipulating things or carrying out the actions shown on the film. Sometimes the action was out of doors, as in the case of many items for the unit 'Trees'. Sheila and I will never forget the sequence where she had to run under the shelter of a tree, and kept running for the sake of the film, despite losing her sandals in mud two feet thick. We only ever found one sandal; the Project Director allowed replacement under the heading of 'photographic materials'! (Harlen, 1975, out of print)

So how useful were the test results after all that effort? The answer is, not very. It is easy with hindsight and after much further experience of evaluation of innovations to explain why. So much depended on the teacher and the previous science experience of the children. Some of our trial teachers were the enthusiasts who had been introducing science into their classrooms anyway. So their children scored initially quite highly on the tests and appeared to make only modest progress when re-tested. Other classes had had no science previously; their initial scores were low and they appeared to make a greater improvement. Thus the change in test scores was no guide to the quality of the classroom experience during the trial.

No adjustment of scores made the picture any clearer; there were just too many uncontrollable variables. So it was not really possible to identify the success of different draft units and parts of units from the results for different questions.

What turned out to be the most useful results for guiding revision of the drafts came from classroom observations – and particularly from talking with children – and teachers' feedback in the questionnaires. We used class observations not only to see what went well and what not so well, but to judge the extent to which the teacher was implementing the 'spirit' of the material. We could then look at their comments knowing whether or not these arose from a serious attempt to try out the approach.

Learning from experience

Fortunately the trials and their evaluation were not one-off events, but in fact took place in four sets. So it was possible to learn from experience and try different approaches to evaluation as well as to writing units. For trials of later units, I developed a list of what came to be called 'diagnostic statements' for teachers to use to look for progress in their children in a wide range of skills, ideas and attitudes. The intention was to help teachers use the observations which they daily make of their children to notice and record whether or not behaviours indicating development were being displayed. Teachers were asked to use these at the start of the trials and again at the end. The statements were cross-referenced to the Science 5/13 objectives so that teachers had some indication of what children had and had not achieved and could use this information in adjusting activities to promote progress. Looking back, this could be seen as an early attempt at formative assessment, using teachers' own judgements. At the time, the statements needed more development and teachers needed more support in both gathering and making use of the information. The challenge to improve the approach and to provide the necessary help was taken up in the later project, Progress in Learning Science.

The evaluation of later trials also attempted to identify changes in teachers' attitudes to the Science 5/13 pedagogy as a result of using trial units. Whilst there were positive changes from pre- to post-trial measures on what was called a 'teachers' preferences' form, these were no greater than might be expected when such a measurement is repeated. It was concluded that using the materials *per se* was not enough to change teachers' attitudes to the methods embodied in the materials. Again, with hindsight this seems obvious, for we know that new material on its own does not necessarily change practice. But it is perhaps only through being alerted by such findings, negative though they may seem, that curriculum and professional developers have worried about and investigated how to bring about changes in teaching approaches.

Was it all worth while?

The fact that early materials, such as Science 5/13, are no longer used – and indeed were only ever used in about 25% of schools – is often taken as a sign of their failure. But that ignores the developmental nature of educational practice. As I think some of this story shows, Science 5/13 not only published a creative and well-tested collection of classroom ideas that have been recycled in many sets of later materials, but fore-warned of fundamental issues in making changes in practice that are still alive in current debate. It broke new ground which has since been cultivated by later genera-tions of projects. If it had not happened, we would not be where we are now. And wasn't it great to be there!

Reference

Harlen, W. (1975) *Science 5/13: a formative evaluation*. London: Macmillan Education.

Sheila Jelly taught science for many years in schools and colleges of higher education in the UK and abroad, researched and wrote extensively on science education and was a member of the Schools Council Science 5/13 Project team.

Questioning and minibeasts

I first became interested in questioning in science when, as a relatively inexperienced secondary-trained teacher, I was appointed to the science department of a college of education and asked to organise a science course for intending primary school teachers. It was a challenging and somewhat daunt-ing task and as part of my preparation I read all I could find about primary science. In the early 60s there was a dearth of publications but in one written by Albert James I found a useful analysis of different kinds of questions and their significance in teaching. In particular I noted his distinction between the unanswerable (If God made the universe who made God?) and the answerable by reference or activity. This writing had a strong resonance with my emerging personal philosophy of science teaching and since that time I have emphasised the importance of questioning, both in my writing and in numerous teachers' courses in the UK and overseas.

I was initially concerned with questions that promoted investigation activity, but following Wynne Harlen's lead I became increasingly interested in ques-tioning to elicit children's ideas. It is in this context that I share one of my favourite anecdotes. It arose from my experience as an Ofsted Inspector observing a group of 6-year-old children exploring the properties of food materials. When the activity was finished I approached one little girl who had worked with great enthusiasm and said, *'You enjoyed that, didn't you?' 'Yes'*, she replied immediately. In an attempt to analyse her learning, I asked, *'Can you say why?'* She looked at me quizzically for a while and then responded hesitantly, *'Y'*. So much for a professional life-time with a focus on effective questioning!

In 1967 (as Sheila Parker) I was a member of the Science 5/13 team writing a book for teachers to help children learn about invertebrate animals. I pondered its title for a long time because I felt that 'Invertebrates' was off-putting and 'Creepy Crawlies' inappropriate. Eventually, as this was the time of the first 'mini-skirts', I decided to call the book 'Minibeasts' and since that time the word has become commonplace.

I well remember the pleasures of working with teachers throughout the country and the excitement of sifting through children's work for examples to include in the book. One piece was memorable, although not published. It said, *'We looked for minibeasts in the graveyard. We didn't find any but we came back and wrote about it.'* This lad may have had underdeveloped observational skills but what an honest recording!

Sheila Jelly

The Assessment of Performance Unit

Extracts from the results of the APU surveys of children at age 11, 1980/81

The following extracts, based on full reports on surveys of children aged 11, are from the Assessment of Performance Unit, *Science report for teachers: 1* (Dept of Education and Science, Welsh Office and Dept of Education for Northern Ireland; HMSO, 1983)

Principal author, **Wynne Harlen** (with Paul Black, Sandra Johnson and David Palacio)

EDITORS' NOTE

These extracts are included because the research carried out by the APU had an important influence on teachers' perceptions of children's responses in primary science. The results encouraged all of us with a particular interest (e.g. Science Co-ordinators) to observe our own practice in the classroom and think how we could improve it.

In 1980 and 1981, the Assessment of Performance Unit carried out the first of a series of surveys in England, Wales and Northern Ireland designed to assess children's performance in science at the age of 10–11 years. This paper presents a summary of the main findings which are likely to be of interest to teachers and some conclusions drawn from them which have implications for practice.

The view of primary science which the surveys attempt to reflect is that it is:
• a rational way of finding out about the world, involving the development of a

willingness and ability to see and use evidence;
• the gradual building of a framework of concepts which help to make sense of experience;
• the fostering of skills and attitudes necessary for investigation and experimentation.
    Practical tests were used to give information about the children's:
• ability to perform investigations;
• skill in observing;
• ability to use simple measuring instruments and equipment;
• reactions to science-based activities.
    Written tests were used to assess the children's ability to:
• plan investigations;
• interpret and explain information given in the question, by making use of patterns in the data or suggesting hypotheses;
• use graphs, tables and charts.

When children carry out practical tests, it is possible to observe what they can actually do rather than what they can express in writing. Thus special importance is attached to these results.

Main findings
Children's performance

MOST 11-YEAR-OLDS:

set about practical investigations in a relevant manner;

observed the broad similarities and differences between objects;

read the scales of simple measuring instruments correctly;

classified objects on the basis of observed properties;

read information from flow charts, tables, pie charts and isolated points from line graphs.

ABOUT HALF 11-YEAR-OLDS:

reported results consistent with the evidence from their investigations;

were more fluent at observing differences than similarities between objects;

made predictions based on observations;

suggested controls in planning parts of investigations;

used given information to make reasonable predictions;

applied science concepts to solve problems;

proposed alternative hypotheses to explain a given phenomenon;

added information to a partially completed graph or chart.

FEW 11-YEAR-OLDS:

repeated measurements or observations to check results;

controlled variables necessary to obtain good quantitative results;

recorded the observation of fine detail of objects;

observed the correct sequence of events;

produced an adequate plan for a simple investigation;

gave good explanations of how they arrived at predictions;

described patterns in observations or data in terms of general relationships.

Children's reactions

In practical tests the children showed that they like and are interested in science activities. They were very willing to be involved in all types of investigations with both living and non-living things. They appeared equally willing to tackle written tests. On the other hand, there was little evidence of children considering their own work in a critical, reflective way.

The survey suggested that, at this age, differences in performance between the sexes were not marked and did not follow a clear pattern. Girls were slightly ahead in using graphs, tables and charts and in making observations of similarities and differences. They were also better at planning investigations and in recording descriptions of events during investigations. This could be related to girls' greater fluency in written language at this age. Boys, on the other hand, were ahead in using measuring instruments, in applying physical science concepts to problems and in recording quantitative results in investigations.

Provision for science activities

85% of schools included science activities in the curriculum, spending, on average, about 5% of lesson time on them. An impression of the material resources available to support the work may be gained from the information that schools spend an average of 5% of their capitation on science. About 50% of the schools ... reported that a member of staff had a post of responsibility for science. Most schools organised the work so that all of the children in a class were engaged on science activities at the same time, though working in groups and often on different problems.

Examples of test questions/practical investigations

Six practical investigations were used in each survey ... In one activity, the pupil was given 3 balls and asked to find out how well the balls bounced on different surfaces. In another, the children had to use their sense of touch to identify pieces of material (glass, metal, wood, leather and rubber). In another example, each pupil was asked to investigate animal preferences for habitat areas (snails and woodlice in light/dark, dry/damp).

In each case, the tester would help the pupil to try things out and, when satisfied that the pupil had understood the problem, the practical work began. The tester would observe the child, using a checklist to note features of the general approach, the attention to variables, and the recording of results. The tester would then discuss the investigation with the pupil to clarify some aspects of what he or she had done.

Summary of implications

... there is a need to consider how to help children to acquire those more specific science skills such as defining patterns in observations, giving explanations, predicting, hypothesising, controlling variables and planning investigations, in which children are less competent ...

These skills are more likely to be developed if teachers have them firmly in mind when planning their work and their daily interactions with children ...

In planning science activities it is necessary to consider how these process skills will be introduced to the children at various ages and stages of development and to decide what progression can be expected as children gain experience.

Planning must also take account of the teaching approaches which will be used to develop science process skills, since these can only be acquired if the children are given opportunities to use them.

10 Primary science – evolution or revolution?

Roy Richards

From Nuffield Junior Science to the National Curriculum

Roy Richards is well known to primary school teachers for his *Early Start* series of books published by Simon and Schuster. He has been a teacher and a senior lecturer at Battersea College of Education and the University of London, Goldsmiths' College. Working for the Schools Council, he was research associate at Bristol University with the Science 5/13 Project (1968–72) and Director of the Learning Through Science Project (1978–84) at Goldsmiths' College. As a long-time member of the ASE, he has served on several of its committees and was reviews editor of *Primary Science Review* from 1985 to 1995. He is a past chairman of the ASE London Region.

Casting my mind back over the century that ASE (or its forerunners) has existed, it is striking to consider the things that must have affected members of the Association and the children they taught: the introduction of film, radio and television, two world wars, the breakthroughs in medicine, especially the discovery of penicillin, the advent of nuclear power, and the changes that have come with our technological age and its rapid embracing of global communication.

The first ASE members would have seen Edward VII ascend the throne in an age when children were educated in Board Schools. Children were taught basic elementary skills to fit them for the economic pattern of the time. The result was a stereo-typed, utilitarian and limited curriculum where children were taught only as much as they needed for the life to which they had been born. Laurie Lee wrote of his school in the novel *Cider with Rosie*: '*We learnt nothing abstract or tenuous here – just simple patterns of facts and letters, portable tricks of calculation, no more than was needed to measure a shed, write a bill, read a swine disease warning.*'

Making the case for science

I came into the ASE in the early 1960s, after the Second World War, when comprehensive schools had already emerged and primary schools were making changes that stemmed, almost inadvertently, from the Hadow Report of 1926. This was entitled *The education of the adolescent*, illustrating that the interest then was not with younger children but with older ones. The school-leaving age was 14 and it was thought proper to have at last three years of secondary schooling. An age break was set at 11 years of age and the primary school was born.

The Second World War slowed down the development of primary education. But, by the time I came on the scene, the need for a more flexible and adaptable labour force, coupled with more forward thinking, had resulted in a change in educational goals. Teachers wanted to give children insight, to enable them to look at things with a critical eye. As a young training-college lecturer I was launched into a world of educational terms: integrated day, vertical grouping, open-plan, discovery learning. Since my specialism was science I looked to those who spoke with authority on this subject. I was impressed by the address that Nathan Isaacs gave to the British Association for the Advancement of Science in 1961 (Isaacs, 1962). It was called 'The case for bringing science into the primary school' and is, to this day, the most powerfully argued and succinct rationale for the scientific education of young children. The School Natural Science Society, with its practical, helpful advice on exploring the natural world, and the National Froebel Association which, amongst other things, brought the wider significance of Piaget's work to notice, made an impression too.

The 1960s were a time of interest in the scientific education of young children and, most importantly, a time when there was motivation to educate children through the world around them. Yet, attentive lecture audiences of teachers and headteachers, although taken with what children could achieve through primary science education, were reluctant to give more than tokenism to work in school. Science was considered an 'extra'. It could be part of the curriculum but in practice it did not usually appear. Headteachers and teachers still needed convincing of the case for science in primary schools.

The ASE played its part. I still possess a series of booklets produced by the Primary Schools Science Committee in 1966. These state the case for 'Science for primary schools' and list useful books, teaching aids, materials, equipment and the use of broadcasts (Primary Schools Science Committee, 1966). The erstwhile Ministry of Education took a lead with an excellent summer school for teachers and other educators. The thought that science could be firmly rooted in primary practice began to take hold and influential voices promulgated its acceptance.

Establishing the philosophical basis

Part of the explosiveness and excitement of the permissive, swinging '60s became apparent in a science education programme – the Nuffield Science Teaching Project – generously funded by Lord Nuffield. As the project successfully developed its secondary schemes, it was decided that there would be a Nuffield Junior Science Project too. Here, a general educational philosophy based on harnessing children's natural curiosity and love of asking questions came into effect. Observations of children learning, both in the classroom and out of it, resulted in almost 40 case studies of work done in schools. These gave a picture of primary science throughout the country. The studies, coupled with helpful source books on apparatus, and animals and plants, presented a liberal, thoughtful, child-centred approach to science in tune with the Plowden Report of that time (Nuffield Junior Science, 1967). Here, with the Nuffield Junior Science Project's substantive account of current practice, was something to build on.

It was quickly followed by one of the first new Schools Council projects, Science 5/13, of which I was a team member. The project's initial concern was to produce a detailed specification of why science should be taught in primary school. After much thought and interaction with children and teachers throughout the country, the book *With objectives in mind* was published (Science 5/13, 1972). Here, for the first time, was a thorough statement about the broad aims of carrying out science with young children and a breakdown of these aims into developmental stages, loosely based on Piagetian principles. The Science 5/13 Project also produced over 20 books describing subject areas in which children were likely to conduct investigations. These texts now form part of the standard practice of science in primary schools, ranging from the *Early experiences* of the infant school, the ever-faithful, but then new, primary topic of *Ourselves* through to *Minibeasts*, the name inspired by the mini-skirt of that era, that has now entered the lexicon of primary science language. The creation of these 20 or so books established a repertoire of experiences to put before children. You cannot implement a philosophy of approach without a practical basis to establish it on.

Nailing down the reasons for primary science practice in this specific way had taken time to happen, dependent as it was on observations of the good practice that had been going on in schools for some years. Thus, it seems, the arrival of primary science was an evolutionary process.

The practicalities

The ASE, as always, continued its work. The Primary Science Sub-Committee of the 1970s, chaired by Dr Margaret Collis, looked at the role of the headteacher and the role of the post-holder for science. It produced helpful influential papers which focused on the practicalities of implementing science in primary schools (Primary Science Sub-Committee, 1974, 1976).

From the late 1970s through to 1984 I directed the Schools Council Learning Through Science Project. It was clear that although the reasons for doing science in primary schools had emerged and were by then well-rehearsed, and whilst there was a clear repertoire of experience to put before children, still far too little science was going on in primary schools. The obvious way forward was for schools to formulate and implement a policy for science, but what should that policy be? The project team wrote a draft document entitled *Towards a school policy for science in primary schools*. This was sent to over 50 local education authorities and groups throughout the country. It had a dual purpose: firstly, to stimulate these groups into looking at practice in their own regions and to plan for it; and, secondly, to provide feedback which the project team could use to suggest a strategy for forming a school policy for science. It is strange to think, when nowadays Ofsted inspectors examine school policies, that back in the 1980s forming one for science should seem such a novel idea. The result of the consultation was the book, *Formulating a school policy* (Learning Through Science, 1980). The project also added to the repertoire of work available by producing 12 units of pupil material. With hindsight these can be seen to cover much of the work in the National Curriculum. They even venture into the then new areas of *Sky and space* and *Earth* (Learning Through Science, 1982, 1983). In this evolutionary process of development the project led the way onward. Discussions about the importance of content in primary science were beginning to appear on the agenda.

Primary science established at last

By the mid-1980s, there was a substantial body of published material on primary science. This had come from national projects, organisations such as the ASE and the Open University, individuals and groups, not to mention the DES and the Assessment of Performance Unit. In 1980 the ASE began its newsletter, *ASE Primary Science*, and in the summer of 1986 launched the, then termly, journal, *Primary Science Review*. This quickly developed into a substantive publication published five times a year, which has gone from strength to strength into this new millennium.

Primary Science Review witnessed the establishment of the National Curriculum and has monitored and reflected upon all the changes in primary science education since. Primary science came into its own at last – a compulsory element of a national curriculum. Pioneering work had made it clear that science was a key subject. That the National Curriculum for primary science could be implemented with relative ease, without revolution, says much for all the work that had gone before.

Why we should carry out primary science, what we should do, how we should do it and how we should evaluate it has come through 100 years of change. This evolution has accelerated as the century progressed and moved into a highly scientific and technological age. The ASE can be proud of the part it has played and continues to play in advancing change and forwarding the scientific education of children.

Many, many happy returns ASE on this your hundredth birthday!

The first issue of *Primary Science Review* published in summer 1986

References

Hadow Report (1926) *The education of the adolescent*. London: HMSO.

Isaacs, N. (1962) The case for bringing science into the primary school. In *The place of science in primary education*. pp. 4–22. British Association for the Advancement of Science.

Learning Through Science (1980) *Formulating a school policy*. London: Macdonald Educational.

Learning Through Science (1982) *Sky and space*. London: Macdonald Educational.

Learning through Science (1983) *Earth*. London: Macdonald Educational.

Nuffield Junior Science (1967):

   Teacher's Guide 1

   Teacher's Guide 2

   Animals and plants: a source book of information and ideas

   Apparatus: a source book of information and ideas

London: Collins.

Primary Schools Science Committee (1966) Science for Primary Schools:

   1. *Children learning through science*

   2. *List of books*

   3. *List of teaching aids*

   4. *Material and equipment*

   5. *Using broadcasts*

Cambridge: Association for Science Education.

Primary Science Sub-Committee (1974) Science and Primary Education. *Paper 1, The role of the headteacher*.

Primary Science Sub-Committee (1976) Science and Primary Education. *Paper 2, A post of responsibility*.

Science 5/13 (1972) *With objectives in mind*. London: Macdonald Educational.

11 *Innovation and experimentation*

Eric Parkinson

Science and technology in the 1970s – a school perspective

Eric Parkinson has taught science and technology in schools and colleges in the UK and abroad. He has been an enthusiastic researcher and supporter in developing primary teachers' scientific and technological expertise. He has worked on many major overseas development projects, such as Technoscience 2000+, the EU Comenius Project, the Success with Science Project, Teacher Opportunities Programme Project (South Africa) and the PROMAT Project. These have involved the creative design of distance-learning programmes and Internet-led INSET. Eric currently lectures in science education at Canterbury Christ Church University College.

Editors' note

Eric Parkinson's contribution illustrates the sense of freedom and excitement we felt in the 1970s at the development of science. His own teaching reflects the close connections between learning science and learning technology (or design and technology). In the 1970s and early 1980s, those of us in primary education believed strongly in the importance of productive links between the two disciplines. Indeed, the initial drafts written by the National Curriculum Working Party for Science included science and technology in the primary years. The two were separated after protests from the secondary school technology teachers. There are many advantages to having separate disciplines in the secondary phase, perhaps fewer at primary level. One particular disadvantage is that learning at the primary stage does not happen in discrete packages; another is that when curriculum areas are separated, it is often harder to encourage positive linkages later on. Eric shows how the issues current in the 1970s inspired relevant problem-solving activities, the fascination of the children and their successful achievements and how his own perception of children's learning was informed by research at that time.

Returning to the UK in the mid-1970s from teaching in the West Indies, I brought with me, not unexpectedly, a taste for things connected with the sea. Whether it was a perception of seemingly blue skies and calm seas that influenced me I am not sure, but one outcome of this strong affinity was a desire to own and live on a boat. This was to have a lucky impact on my first teaching post in the UK and to influence subsequent developments. I say 'lucky' because my choice of school was most influenced by its location – it would be chance if I found myself in a 'good' school, let alone one with science in the curriculum.

A survey of the English coast suggested that an estuary would be a good place to own a boat, and amongst the applications sent off to schools in coastal towns was one to a primary school in Strood, Kent, on the banks of the River Medway.

My application was successful and I started teaching at Elaine Junior School. I soon discovered that the lower reaches of the Medway were an historic rather than a picturesque stretch of river. Under the wintry grey skies of north Kent, the initial enthusiasm for a boat waned somewhat. A conventional life ashore replaced the dream of a life on the high seas. However, this was in part offset by the character of Elaine Junior School. This was no run-of-the-mill primary school: it was a large school and it had a 'reputation'. In the days before I arrived, it had become significant in curriculum development in primary mathematics.

Under the leadership of headteacher Arthur Ashton, this pattern was now repeating itself with primary science. I suppose, in modern parlance, we would refer to such an establishment as a 'beacon' school. It was something of a pioneer in terms of pushing out the boundaries of children's experience in science, and drawing upon the wider curriculum to achieve this.

In this new millennium, we have a national curriculum which not only specifies what to teach, but increasingly how to teach. In the 1970s this was not the case. As a result, the curriculum was fluid enough to embrace many ideas from teachers and children alike. At Elaine Junior School, staff were encouraged to extend their skills and experiment. These were exciting times.

Cross-curricular approach

A cross-curricular approach to learning was encouraged, with various topics cross-cutting areas such as maths, history, geography and, of course, science. For my own part, I remember in particular that 'making things', or 'technology', could play a useful part in children's learning, especially in relation to science. This initial notion of 'technology' was in later years refined to become 'design and technology'. In these early days, there was no need to distinguish 'information technology', since the world of education was yet to be invaded by personal computers.

Why was technology so important? First, from the children's perspective, it was fun. There is a hunger for practical activity which can be well met by 'making things'. Second, from a teaching position, as I was discovering, technology was a useful vehicle from which to take children's learning into science. It provided everyday, realistic contexts as conceptual platforms from which children could seamlessly move from the made world into the question-raising and observation that drives science.

Mangonels and land yachts

Technology not only provided everyday contexts from the real, made world, it could take us into the past too. I remember well a history topic, the focus of which was 'Life in Mediaeval times'. The technology of siege warfare provided a suitable context for the modelling of catapults and other devices. This led on to discussions about force and energy, and consideration of the appropriateness of materials for various purposes based upon their characteristics. The children could have modelled their ideas through balsa wood craft. They did not. Instead, some rather large saplings in a somewhat overgrown corner of the school grounds were cut down and used as constructional timber for, as far as the children were concerned, real ballistas and mangonels. These were the days of freedom and experimentation. Not a risk-assessment form was in sight as lumps of brick hurtled across the school grounds with gasps from the assembled crowd. And nobody got hurt.

Similarly, life-sized modelling enabled children to build a land yacht capable of carrying a child across a playground on a windy day. For this experience a 'grown-up' construction kit called Handy Angle was used. I have no doubt that the manufacturers of this product – built to make shelves and racking in warehouses – would have been fascinated to see it used in a school environment.

Investigating alternative energy sources

I recall too, showing the children a film (video was yet to make significant impact in primary classrooms) on so-called 'alternative energy'. This American production was made, I think, immediately in the wake of the mid-1970s oil crisis. It was a strange film that depicted the exponents of alternative energy as hippies living out some alternative lifestyle in a commune with windmills and solar water-heaters. I suspect it was a rather tacky attempt to discredit those who had chosen to live low-impact, low-energy lives, and paint them as un-American subversives. Environmental concerns had yet to become focused by the notion of 'global warming'.

But back to the film. The children were fascinated, and not only by the southern drawl of the hippies. We made prototype solar water-heaters out of glass tubes covered with aluminium foil and painted black. Children logged performance data in different solar conditions. There was a perfect blend of technology leading to science. Children 'made things' and then raised questions about their performance. They put forward hypotheses about the values of solar energy and predicted what temperatures would be attained in sunny and cloudy conditions. They had to keep accurate records and assemble data in a systematic way. Above all else, discussions clarified and extended thinking, not only for the children but for me too. Further experiment led to investigations on the use of different colours as backgrounds for absorbing solar radiation.

We moved on from solar water-heaters to waterwheels and wind-turbines. Tin cans were cut with tin snips to be assembled as paddles for a waterwheel. This great creation, with masses of sharp edges, fixed to a timber frame, was duly taken along on a residential visit to a field study centre. In the dark confines of Angley Wood in the Weald of Kent, a small stream was harnessed to provide an unusual way of lifting up children. A piece of heavy cord was tied to the waterwheel shaft, slung over an overhanging branch and a child attached. The child was then dragged upward and outward over the stream. Lifting the waterwheel clear of the water, we were able to halt this upward climb before child and branch became rather messily entangled.

The wind-turbine was an equally impressive construction. It was composed of a bicycle wheel upon which long pieces of plastic cut from corrugated roofing sheet had been attached as blades. This produced a magnificent beast with outstretched, swishing yellow fingers which would turn in the slightest breeze. Of course, it had to be a useful machine, so a large loop of elastic was stretched around the rim to act as a belt to drive a small dynamo of the type used for powering lights on bicycles. Simple circuits had even more meaning now that children could generate their own electric currents.

Disaster eventually struck when the turbine was taken outside in somewhat gusty conditions and children became unhappy with the merry whine the blades were making as the rotor spun ever-faster. On a sudden gust, the whole machine was uprooted, the rotor striking the ground and thrashing itself to destruction to a mixture of dismay and enjoyment amongst the assembled crowd (situated upwind and at a safe distance, I hasten to add!).

Hot-air balloons

I think the picture I am beginning to paint is one in which novelty and the role of the spectacle were important. Nowhere was this more evident than when hot-air balloons were launched. As part of their mathematical work, some children in the class of a fellow teacher, John Williams, were able to produce a simple net for assembling the envelope for a hot-air balloon. The net was so simple – it involved five sheets of tissue paper – that balloons could be made in a matter of minutes.

With an on-board heat source of flaming cotton wool soaked in methylated spirits, these creations were remarkably stable in flight. Once successfully launched, a balloon could reach significant heights and cover great distances before the flames died down to let a fireless, harmless envelope return to Earth. I remember the sense of shared excitement at launch times.

Children were enthusiastic about events like these and they provided a vivid backdrop to the discussion of scientific ideas. Years later, children returning to the school would refer to these events, which had made an indelible impression upon them. These experiences also drove the wider curriculum through, for example, drama, music and art.

These were times when teachers and children were learning alongside each other. For me, this shared experience was most evident during discussions with children. Here, meanings could be probed and children's ideas unpacked and explored.

Probing misconceptions

Consideration of the children's local environment led to some interesting discussion. Elaine Junior School was situated on former chalk downland overlooking a dry valley leading to the River Medway. This was a fossil landscape, formed in past times of higher rainfall, and now clad with housing. This set of circumstances led to the children arriving at their own explanations of how their local environment had been shaped. What was the shape of the land that led down from the school and then rose up again? The term 'valley' would be offered after some discussion. And how had the valley been made? This was a real problem. The notion that a dry valley could once have been the site of active erosion, when all that could be seen was a sea of houses built over a linear depression in the land, was hardly going to be an idea that children would derive naturally using available evidence.

They suggested that valleys such as this one, which the children walked up and down each day, were dug out. So what happened to the soil that was dug out? Simple – 'It was used to make the hills'. Naive ideas such as this were repeated over and over. For instance, in response to my question about which way the River Medway flowed, children readily told me it went 'from the sea to the land'. And the reason for this? Because there was lots of water 'out there' and it flowed along the river into the land where it eventually sank into boggy places such as marshes or disappeared into little holes called springs.

Later academic study and exposure to research findings (e.g. Nuffield Junior Science) told me that I had been probing what were to become known as children's misconceptions or 'alternative frameworks'. In subsequent years, whole teaching schemes would be founded on these principles.

I raise this issue of children's ideas because it was through experiences such as these that I became convinced of the need for first-hand experience as a means of enabling children to gather their own evidence. Whilst I have depicted what might be regarded as strictly geographical examples above, the issue of first-hand experience shines through. The children needed a range of experiences from which to construct their own explanations and, crucially, they needed some searching questions to un-settle the layers of understanding they were in the process of laying down. In teach-ing terms, the greater their exposure to available evidence, the greater the chance of constructing ideas which accorded more closely to the ideas held by the scientific community.

Curriculum development

If Elaine Junior School was a 'beacon school', then the beckoning light enabled it to come to the attention of, share in, and contribute to curriculum development initia-tives. Through the 1970s and into the 1980s, the publications of the Science 5/13 and Learning Through Science Projects dominated primary science. My colleagues and I at Elaine Junior School were fortunate in being able to participate in trials of these materials. So it was that, in a small way, we were able to contribute to the primary science movement which was gathering speed and spreading in influence across the nation.

Another seminal publication was the inspirational *Science craft* by Keith Geary. This work expressed the fluidity which existed between science and technology in the 1970s. It was full of things to make and try out and was way ahead of its time in terms of the utilisation of scrap/reclaimed materials that has become the mantra of the modern environmental lobby.

My belief in the role of science with and through technology was reinforced by the government policy statement of 1985, *Science 5–16: A statement of policy*. This was an early kind of national curriculum statement for science and technology. It was beautifully simple and stated in very general terms the broad areas of experience which children should have. In particular, it noted that science and technology should be experienced by children 'as a continuum'.

Had this policy been maintained and strengthened we would, I think, have had a very different kind of curriculum from the one that exists today. Subject self-interest was soon to carve up the curriculum into compartments. Cross-curricular approaches became largely unviable in a subject-led approach to teaching. The dominance of scheme-led, acontextual maths and English in rigid, inflexible 'hours' has broken many of the threads of a cross-curricular fabric into which a broader understanding of the world can be woven.

On reflection, I think it would be a mistake to regard the 1970s as a 'golden age' for primary science (and technology!). Children were often exposed to a series of experiences which did not build up a coherent framework for understanding. Progression and continuity were not generally evident in planning from class to class and scientific skills were misunderstood by many teachers who were unfamiliar with or even disliked science.

However, these were times of innovation and experimentation. Boundaries had not yet been set and new territory could readily be explored. And believe me it was!

12 Teaching infants and influencing national policy

Audrey Randall

The joys of teaching the early years and the trials and tribulations of getting our message across

Audrey Randall spent a few years in scientific occupations (laboratory researcher, dental nurse, etc.) before going into teaching. She enthusiastically embraced science education, specialised in early childhood development and became a headteacher in Hertfordshire. She joined the ASE Primary Science Sub-Committee, became the editor of the ASE broadsheet, *ASE Primary Science*, as well as representing the ASE on parliamentary select committees. She was a member of the original working party for the National Curriculum for Science, a moderator for key stages 1 and 2 assessment and a supervisory tutor in initial teacher education.

My early years in teaching

Nothing was further from my thoughts when I left school in the mid-1940s than that I would one day become a teacher. My schooling, prior to and during the Second World War, had been disrupted, with many people joining the armed forces. Most of the teachers I encountered at the three schools I attended represented a 'force majeur' of angry, frustrated women who shouted at me most of the time. They had eagle eyes which never missed a movement; they instructed rather than taught and many of them did not appear to like children.

There were a few jewels in the crown that I fondly remember: one of them was the science teacher at Enfield County School for Girls. She smiled, allowed questions, explained without making us feel foolish *and* she let us 'do' things. We studied 'general science' in those days and years later I always felt that it had given me a very good basic foundation in the subject.

Twenty years later, in the mid-1960s when my own children were at school, teachers were more approachable. They smiled, talked to the children as if they were people and seemed to enjoy working alongside their pupils. Not all the teachers I met then were like that, but certainly a great many more than when I went to school. Their approach, which made learning an exciting experience for children, motivated me to register as a mature student in a teacher training college in 1964.

Learning to teach as a mature student

I chose to train to teach primary-age children and in addition studied natural history. I thoroughly enjoyed college, though it was hard work with a young family and husband to look after. (Yes, in those days, women were still expected to 'look after' their husbands. He was, after all, the 'breadwinner'.) As a mature student, I was awarded a grant and I thought I was in heaven. I thoroughly enjoyed every minute and felt enormously privileged to have the chance to go to college.

The education course was brilliant. It totally reinforced my own experiences of bringing up a family: learning about child development, giving children first-hand experiences, encouraging them to ask questions and helping them to find out about the world in which they live. I went on to teach in an infant school in a rather challenging area with children from a wide range of backgrounds, which gave me ample opportunity to put my philosophy of education into practice in the real world.

Learning where eggs come from

The headteacher at this school encouraged us to let children explore using all their senses and I was in my element. Many of the children lived in flats, were not allowed to keep pets and had no gardens. We felt that the school could help to fill this void in

5-year-old children feeding the school pets (Brookland Infant School, Cheshunt, Herts 1984)

the children's experience so we kept ducks, chickens and rabbits. Many of the children had no idea that chickens and ducks laid eggs. They constantly told me that their mums got real eggs from Tesco's. The children shared responsibility for looking after the school pets and nothing will ever take away the pleasure of seeing the look of joy and wonder on their faces when they collected the eggs which they used later to make cakes.

The young Icarus!

Each class also had a small garden plot to look after and children's own ideas for growing things and other scientific enquiries were positively encouraged. I remember one boy, Stephen, in particular. He was 6 years old and had been talking about Icarus with his grandfather. He decided to make himself some wings to see if he could fly like Icarus. My agreement and support disguised the concern I felt at what he might not be able to achieve. He spent a lot of time making wings of different shapes and thicknesses. He then devised a test to try to prove that he could fly. He jumped from a low wall and measured the distance he had travelled, first without his wings and then with his wings. He said that he had jumped further with his wings so he must have flown.

A little while later, he told me that he had tried harder when he had his wings on, so it was not a fair test. He then tested himself against a friend, he with his wings on and his friend Mark without wings. Again, Stephen jumped further with the wings, so he said he could fly, but later, again, he said he could jump further than Mark anyway so it was not a fair test.

Stephen was beginning to understand about fair tests and controlling variables. I have always felt that it is essential for children to learn about fair testing by trial and error. Prescriptive science 'recipes' never give that experience; the children follow instructions and reach the expected result – hardly awe-inspiring stuff. They never understand the importance of controlling variables to obtain valid evidence and a justifiable result.

Encouraging careful observation

When I became the headteacher of that same school, we were able to develop the science curriculum even further. We had some wonderful times. We took a lot of trouble encouraging the children to observe carefully and to record what they had found out using whatever medium was appropriate, whether it was a fac-

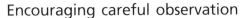

David's drawing of a crane fly

tual report, written work or discussion, a painting or a drawing, a model or a drama. Observation is essential and all too often in this day and age, children want to dash off a quick drawing before moving on to something else. I used to sit with children, like the time when we were looking at crane flies. We talked about them and I asked questions such as: *'Do they have eyes? Do they have knees and shoulders? How many legs have they got?'* When David brought his detailed drawing to me afterwards I was amazed at what he had noticed – and he was justifiably proud of himself.

Further opportunities

In the 1970s I was invited to work with County Science Advisers on their in-service courses (highly rewarding work). Then I was invited to join the ASE Primary Science Sub-Committee, and, although this was quite a challenge, it gave me the opportunity to work with such inspiring people as Margaret Collis, Roy Richards, Doug Kincaid and Helen Rapson. Their enthusiasm and expertise gave me greater confidence to develop the science curriculum in my school.

A *woman's place*

On one occasion, when I was voluntarily helping the Science Advisory Team with in-service courses, I gave an illustrated talk, showing examples of science work from children aged 5–7 years. In the question time that followed, a well-known (then) college lecturer asked me why I did not concentrate my efforts on 'washing nappies' or whatever it was we did in infants schools, rather than waste my time trying to teach science to such young children.

I was greatly incensed by his attitude and comment but, with the support of the Primary Adviser, managed to rise above the insult. Later, however, when the same man had the audacity to publish a scheme of work in science 'for infant children', I did not feel so gracious!

My school as an experimental playground!

I had always encouraged a great diversity of experience in the curriculum and it was rewarding and surprising to see how much children can learn from these experiences. The Science 5/13 team came to my school to trial some of the materials in the unit on plastics. The children knew so much! All their making activities with recycled materials had taught them about the properties of various types of plastics – flexibility, rigidity,

Children aged 5–6 learning through first-hand experience (Brookland Infant School, Cheshunt, Herts 1984)

etc. – and which adhesives held them together.

Our school became something of a testing ground for the national initiatives in primary science: more Science 5/13, Schools Council 'Learning Through Science' and the Match and Mismatch materials. We were supported by our local education authority in self-monitoring, audio-taping ourselves and our children and video-taping ourselves teaching. It was quite disconcerting at times: we were clear about our aims and objectives but we found sometimes that we inhibited the children's learning as much as promoting it. Nevertheless, it was useful in helping us to improve our teaching techniques and, as an outcome of this, in the late 1970s we formed a self-support group (The Longsearch Group) which still meets today to discuss educational issues.

ASE Primary Science Committee

The sudden disbanding of the ASE Primary Science Sub-Committee in 1979, without a reason being given, was upsetting, as we had worked so hard and published valued books, such as *The role of the headteacher* and *A post of responsibility*. Happily, demand from the primary members influenced the ASE to set up a full Primary Science Committee, later that year. Helen Rapson was asked to edit a termly broadsheet called *ASE Primary Science* – the very first publication for primary schools to come from the ASE (*Primary Science Review* followed in 1986). *ASE Primary Science* used children's work to illustrate teaching and learning in science and was sold in bulk to LEAs for distribution to schools. At one time, over 30,000 copies were sold. I was thrilled to join Helen's Advisory Editorial Board and even more so when work from my school went into the first edition of *ASE Primary Science*. I became the editor for 10 years after Helen Rapson retired and the broadsheet is now regularly included in copies of *PSR*. It still aims to show children's work as good examples of classroom science.

Influencing Government policy

In the 1980s I was seconded for a year to evaluate the recent Government initiative for maths and science, with ESG funds (Education Support Grants). Although it was a very wide-ranging and valuable experience for me, I had concerns about the approaches used by some individuals or authorities. In some cases, the initiative relied on the cascade model of teaching methods and curriculum content – not always a successful way of training teachers unless long-term funding is made available. My concerns were reinforced when most of the funding was withdrawn in 1988–89.

In 1985, as part of a panel of ASE representatives, we met the Select Committee for Science Education at the Houses of Parliament to convince them that science should be given the status of a 'core' subject in the forthcoming National Curriculum. I was ill-prepared for this ordeal. We were given a very short briefing about the procedures and told that questions would be put to the chairman of our panel who would then choose the most appropriate person to respond. I don't remember what was said but we must have been pretty persuasive – science became a core subject.

Towards the end of the summer term of 1987, I was talking to teachers at the Cambridge Institute of Education. I remember being very flippant when teachers asked me about assessing children in science but, as I drove home, I began to wonder if there would be 'tests' for young children in the future. About 10 minutes after I got home, the telephone rang and a cultured voice said, '*Mrs Randall? Mrs Audrey Randall? The Secretary of State, Mr Kenneth Baker, is inviting you to be on the Science Working Group for the National Curriculum.*' Well, as you can imagine, I thought I was being set up by some of the teachers with whom I had been flippant in the afternoon. So I said, '*Stop mucking about! Who is it?*' The caller gave her name and repeated the invitation.

I was amazed. I had had no idea that this sort of approach would be used. I said I was not sure, what would it entail? I was informed that most meetings would be held after school, at weekends or in the school holidays. There would be no pay for the extra time involved but travel expenses (or any in-school supply cover needed) would be paid by my local authority. I was given one hour to make my decision. That was enough time for two strong cups of tea. Then I accepted (and phoned my Chair of Governors and local Chief Education Officer for their permission).

I am giving these details so the reader may know about how policy documents are sometimes prepared. The workload was massive; we had to write a national curriculum for science starting from blank pages in less than nine months. We were lucky in that our group was so positive; we had great rapport and a wonderful leader in Jeff Thompson. What shocked me was everyone's assumption that we should write a 'top-down' model. I had naively assumed that education begins with children at age 5 and builds up from there. At that time, primary science was taught in an integrated way within the context of a themed approach and children were given several opportunities to revisit ideas in as many ways as possible, spread over several sessions. Now when I look at the programmes of study, I see that children have one or two short controlled science sessions per week, with science often isolated from the rest of the curriculum. Although science is a compulsory subject in schools, I fear we have lost a lot of the awe, understanding, wonder and fun. Today's approach is reminiscent of the 1930s when the focus was teaching the curriculum, rather than teaching the children.

In spite of my reluctance to join the NC Working Group and its top-down model, I am still glad of my involvement. For me, there were also many disappointments and shock at my colleagues' lack of understanding of teaching and learning in the early years. Secondary colleagues could not comprehend children who learn in a holistic way. They could not understand the implications of testing 7-year-old children, some of whom had been in nursery and infants schools (with, say, 15 terms of formal education), while others had entered mainstream school on their fifth birthday (say 5 terms only). None of us who argued the pros and cons of systematic assessment would have believed that, a few years later, schools themselves would be judged by the levels of attainment of their pupils, let alone that children would be assessed at the age of 5. I do not believe that any method of assessing children or schools which is rushed into place at such a speed can be properly effective, fair or productive. What was worse was the attitude of the Secretary of State and his Minister for Education. Their politics dominated the agenda rather than the professional expertise of the educators. We were all giving up our time and energy to the project, often to the detriment of our own personal lives, and yet we were treated churlishly and patronisingly. Fortunately, we had a gracious and diplomatic chairman in Jeff Thompson, else we might have abandoned the work.

Sorry, Minister!

Some of my experiences working on the National Curriculum were rather more amusing. In June 1988, at the final meeting of the Science Working Group for the National Curriculum, Colin Smith, a headteacher and member of the group, presented us all with an 'elephant ear pot' made by the children at his primary school. I was rushing to catch a flight from Newcastle to London, so I quickly packed the pot in a plastic bag with my washing. Also in my travel bag was the final, so far secret, draft of the National Curriculum for Science. I was accompanied by an official from the Department of Education and Science.

Going through security at Newcastle Airport, my bag caused concern and I was asked what was in it. I explained that the heavy object was 'an elephant pot'. The security guard was not convinced and proceeded to empty all the contents of my bag on to the table. It was most embarrassing to see the pot, the National Curriculum papers and my underwear all in a heap together. To add to my chagrin, the young official travelling with me was carrying his National Curriculum papers in a locked document case with the EIIR insignia on it, securely chained to his wrist!

'Drawing' conclusions?

Since retiring as a headteacher in 1990, I have worked as a moderator for key stages 1 and 2 assessment in state and independent schools, mainstream and special schools and supervising student-teachers. The experience of visiting so many different schools has been a privilege, one I would wish primary classteachers could have. Whilst some in-service courses offer limited opportunities to do this, it cannot be done effectively without proper funding.

Even as a moderator, I could still be surprised by children's responses. Once I was observing key stage 1 assessment tasks (children were assessed in science at KS1 then). I was monitoring a group of 7-year-olds carrying out an investigation about the rate at which water cools. The children had to use a thermometer and record the temperature of the water at 1-minute intervals. The teacher went to get the hot water and said to the children, *'While you are waiting, draw your tables ready to record your results and don't forget to use a ruler.'* The children obediently drew their classroom tables, including the legs, and used a ruler as instructed!

What of the future?

I have also witnessed the changes to the emphases in the curriculum and feel very concerned. Science now seems to be marginalised in many schools. The emphasis on literacy and numeracy, being taught in the morning, sends a strong message to parents and children that science is no longer important. I have seen formal science sessions taught in the afternoon which were so prescriptive that the children were simply following instructions. There seems to be little opportunity for children to explore, investigate their own questions or further their own intellectual development.

I am not, however, totally despondent. I feel confident that science will eventually find its rightful place again. Children will always need first-hand experiences to understand the world in which they live. They will always need to learn 'how to learn' and will not be able to do that if they are talked at rather than participating fully in their own education. Motivating children to learn is the prime objective of every teacher. Let us hope we can do this by bringing back a little more awe and wonder and children's ownership of the science curriculum. I know that the ASE Primary Science Committee 2000, under the chairmanship of Anne Goldsworthy, would support this view for the future.

13 A Welsh perspective

Neville Evans

The National Curriculum, assessment and a love of Sc1

Neville Evans took a degree in physics and then did postgraduate research for his PhD, after which he taught science in secondary schools and physics in higher education in Wales. His main life's work has been as a member of HMI (Wales) from which he retired in 1998. During this time he was closely involved with the implementation of the National Curriculum for Science and with the development of assessment tests for England and Wales (primary and secondary). Neville has maintained close links with the ASE in South Wales and was admitted to life membership in 1999. Sport has featured prominently in his life and cricket is still a passion, although his playing is now wholly in the mind, where he constantly scores admirable centuries and takes impossible catches. Another special interest is choral singing, though for a number of years his involvement has been more in the entrepreneurial mode than the vocal, organising concerts by massed choirs in the prestigious St David's Hall in Cardiff.

Neville retains a keen interest in education. His motivation? Grandchildren.

The eye and the mind

Prior to my joining HMI (Wales), my only experience of primary schools was that of a pupil. My memory retained images of rooms mostly filled with desks (in rows) and some pictures on the walls. It was therefore something of a shock to enter the wonderful worlds of colour to be found in most primary schools. Everywhere – classrooms, foyers, corridors – was filled with colour. Another feature I

Infant class-room wall displaying work on the autumn/ harvest

noticed was that the displays had an educational purpose, namely, to encourage pupils to strive for better presentation and to make the walls into locations for reading and study that complemented the work at the desks (or, more evident by this time, tables).

My early experience on entering secondary schools as an inspector was one of 'no change' from my own pupil days. Rich variety of colour was not a feature. Display, where it occurred, usually had a functional, not educational purpose, namely to cover ugly patches on damp walls. Science laboratories sometimes had colourful wall coverings but it was depressing that so many of them were from commercial enterprises, with print so small and dense that only pupil members of MENSA equipped with binoculars had any hope of learning from them.

I'm glad to say that by my last days as an inspector, most secondary science teachers had learned from their primary colleagues that displayed material can have a potent influence on learning. It is common now for year 7 and 8 pupils to produce posters for display but I have to note, regretfully, that most are on such issues as safety, pollution and wildlife protection. Notwithstanding the worthiness of such issues, I wish that more displays ranged more widely across the curriculum and were more pedagogic in their intent. While I was very happy to see this extension of the visual element into secondary education, it bothered me that little was done in this regard for and by pupils in years 9 to 13. This has always struck me as strange because it is evident that as pupils become older they mature in many ways, not least in skills of graphicacy. I remain convinced that displays by older pupils (not necessarily all) would add distinctive richness to the whole mysterious process of learning.

One final thought on this matter of making laboratories (and classrooms) interesting places to be in. Wouldn't it be enriching to have all school laboratories (and some primary classrooms) named after scientists, some international, some local? There could be a plaque, with notes, on the outside of the door for the benefit of passers-by. I recall posters in the past but they were of scientists long since dead who usually lived and worked far away from most schools. Much like aliens, not humans!

Land of my fathers

For me, working mostly in Wales, a very significant change is the extensive increase in the use of Welsh as the medium of teaching, testing and examining in science in primary and secondary education. This is one of the consequences of the substantial increase in the number of bilingual schools across Wales over the past 40 years. In the 1960s, there were few books of any kind in Welsh, so the task of teachers who wished to use Welsh as the medium was one of voluntary translation or adaptation. Such commitment, far beyond the call of ordinary duty, cannot be costed because it is beyond normal scales of value.

But now, thanks to continuing unstinting efforts of teachers and enlightened support from local and central government, it is possible for pupils from pre-nursery to A-level to pursue their science courses in Welsh and to use colourful books of different kinds. Some books are adaptations of popular English ones, while others are original works.

An interesting aspect of this development has relevance for the teaching and learning of science in any language. Those of us who have been close to this work for many years are familiar with the question: *'Do you have Welsh equivalents for all scientific terms?'* The answer quite simply was and is: *'We have some already, we create some, we borrow some.'* This last activity applies to Welsh as it does to English and French, for instance. That's the thing about languages. They grow. We all owe a considerable debt to the Greeks, not to forget Latin for biology. By the way, we don't translate Latin classifications into Welsh!

For many people, science seems especially linguistically problematic because, so it is thought, its 'technical' (sometimes synonymous for some with 'strange', 'threatening', 'alien') terminology presents insurmountable barriers to understanding. However, a word (technical or not) is simply an item in a person's vocabulary. Whether or not it constitutes a 'threat' to anyone depends on whether or not that person has a meaningful experience to accompany the technical word. Without such experience, the word (any word, all words) is devoid of meaning (e.g. 'force').

In my experience, the language challenge within science is not coping with single technical terms, but having control of the sentences and paragraphs within which such terms are found or are to be placed (e.g. *'May the Force be with you!'* or *'He forced me to go with him'* or *'A force can be a push or a pull'*).

The big C change

The biggest administrative change that occurred in science education in my experience was the coming of the National Curriculum. It was a privilege to be involved in the early stages of its implementation and the development of assessment tests. I was, and remain, an unrepentant supporter of the National Curriculum and of its science element in particular. Despite all the wonderful work of the Nuffield teams in the 1960s and 1970s, and of other curriculum development ventures that followed in the wake of Nuffield, it remains a fact of history that in the 1980s there was not the nationwide endeavour in science that we now have. The National Curriculum was needed; revolution (as it was seen by some) was required because evolution (as was preferred by some, usually the same some) had not worked.

This is not to disparage the efforts made by many before 1989 to improve science education. But there were tracts of desert. Perhaps, as one trained in physics, I was naturally a little disturbed that in primary school the familiar timetable label was Nature Study. I would have settled for The Study of Nature, but what was often presented had no semblance of study to it. It was a gentle wander up the twig, naming parts, and setting up the inevitable nature table, that much revered display of death purporting to be the epitome of biology, the study of life.

The National Curriculum transformed the scene in ways that I do not need to itemise here. I pay tribute to the work of Professor Jeff Thompson and his Working Group. Has the NC blossomed as promised? Who can tell for sure? I have a feeling that science education would be stronger than it is had the NC been left alone to mature by modifications in the light of professional practice. I still like the format of the original seventeen attainment targets (if you've still got a copy, hang on to it!). The compaction from seventeen into four was a retrograde step, promoted and agreed on rather flimsy and ill-articulated arguments concerning assessment.

Testing times

National Curriculum assessment tests still present a huge challenge to all concerned. There remains a real danger that their prominence and substance will cause a damaging conflict (of spirit as much as anything) with the philosophy that underpins the curriculum. I do not have a political or other aversion to testing, but the whole bureaucracy and industry of assessment has become an impediment to improvement of meaningful standards, these being not at all the same as test data. When it comes to worthwhile and contributive assessment, the work of the Assessment of Performance Unit (APU) in the 1980s stands as a beacon to guide us all. We salute the work of Professor Paul Black, Ros Driver and Wynne Harlen. It was another privilege of my career to occasionally have quite close involvement with them and their work.

While I'm reflecting on assessment, testing and examining, I wish to share a real gripe that I have nurtured silently (almost!) over many years. When will we have the courage and insight to abandon levels and grades which bedevil the interpretation of outcomes at 7+, 11+, 14+, 16+ and 18+? My antagonism is strongest at points of transition in the system, at 16+ and 18+, because decisions about life (yes, LIFE) are made on whether or not a student is grade B or grade C and so on. Everybody knows that the difference in performance might be just a single point in a 100-point scale and everybody also knows that no examination or assessment system is accurate to this extent. Individuals and schools are judged on how many level 2s or level 4s or grade Cs they achieve.

My objection is that such gradings (and the levellings at 7+, 11+ and 14+) purport an accuracy which they do not and can not have. My preference is for the 100-point scale (yes, in numbers from 1 to 100) on the grounds that, first, everybody throughout society has some sort of feel for percentages and, second (and much more important), that nobody with any educational sense will 'believe' the apparent, but blatantly absurd, accuracy of the 100-point scale. The consequence would be that anybody who has to deal with such scales will take the particular outcome for a particular student as indicative rather than definitive of performance and potential. What will then happen is the encouragement of good discussion and thought about the best next steps.

Mark my words (and diagrams)

There is obviously a strong case for good assessment and an undoubted need for improving instruments of assessment and means of enabling pupils and students to improve their own work. Science education has not been notable for perceptive marking of written and drawn work, to name the most visible type of assessment. I still recall *'This is a childish diagram'* as the sole comment by a chemistry teacher on the work of a year 7 pupil. At age 11 what else could it be? But is it merely stating the obvious or is it a criticism? If the former, it is irrelevant; if the latter, unhelpful. Science work should be marked first and foremost for its science. That is why it was set. Supportive other comment is also important but not as important.

The problem facing those who wish to advance systems of assessment is to provide a convenient model of progress. Some pioneering work was done on this in the early days of the NC by a small group known by the letters TGAT (Task Group on Assessment and Testing). It was chaired by Paul Black who, before he moved into education research, had had a distinguished career as a university scientist. This background naturally (unwittingly?) persuaded him to present pupil progress in the form of a graph. However, the physicist in him required this graph to be a straight line through the origin, so we had the vision of the inevitable linear rise through the levels (only levels 1–10, remember) of the NC. Of course, as a top-class physicist, Paul had also included ample error bars, so there should have been plenty of scope for the general upward trend of children's progress in science to follow many paths within the bounds of the error bars. Somehow, I do not think that this subtlety was fully appreciated by those who favoured the simplicity of the linear rise (the range of error bars was subsequently omitted in assessments that 'levelled' children's progress).

I have often wondered, especially now when it seems that all educational outcomes are relentlessly on an upward slope, whether the TGAT model for assessment might have been different had the chairman of the group been of a different academic background. Suppose, for an instance, that the individual had been a geographer. Would the model have been a set of contour lines, with level 0 at sea-level and level 10 out of sight in the clouds? I think such a model might have had advantages over the sloping line, even with error bars. For instance, it would have been entirely acceptable for pupils to remain on, say, level 4 (the same contour line) so long as there was evidence that they had moved along the line and experienced the richness of different views. (Younger children, in particular, need considerable experience of scientific ideas in a wide range of contexts before the ideas start to become meaningful.)

Incessant calls for 'better standards' soon became nothing more than frenzied demands for higher scores. In this way they lose that necessary relationship with an understanding of the system which scores or data represent. Only the disciplined pursuit of excellence will lead to an assured improvement of standards.

I love thee, Sc1

Having declared my admiration of the NC, the jewel in the crown for me is Sc1 or attainment target 1. In 1989, it had the title *Exploration of science*. By 1995 it had evolved into *Experimental and investigative science*. In 2000, it is *Scientific enquiry*. No matter about the change of name, I still love it. A rose by any other name ... I am well familiar with the criticisms of it, fair and unfair, but I have never doubted the need for what it represents, namely the alternative to the mindnumbing effect of pointless confirmatory practical work (secondary) or 'reading about it' instead of practical primary science.

This is not the place to rake over cold embers of past fires of debate and argument. I just state my hope that, whatever further curriculum change might occur in the future, Sc1 will remain prominent because, at its best, it is the common essence of all scientific endeavour. It is true that over the past decade the development of Sc1 was hindered by a needlessly bureaucratic approach to assessment. At its best, Sc1 is a vehicle for promoting the thinking faculty of all pupils and for enabling them to appreciate at first hand the nature of scientific knowledge, how it is formed and what it can and cannot offer.

In these days of speedy communication and the curse of the instant comment on a contemporary issue of concern, the ignorance of people ('who should know better') is disturbing, even alarming when they are the people of influence and power in our society. Sc1 has the potential to be an antidote. Within Sc1, since all sciences are so dependent upon data of some controllable and definable kind (most often in the form of numerical measurements), close attention needs to be given to securing in pupils (who become 'the public') a good understanding of what significance can be attached to data and any claimed or discernible trends in sets of data.

Precision impossible

Of crucial importance, but unthinkingly neglected over the past century of school science, is the need to obliterate the notion that exactness is possible in any physical measurement. This notion amounts to a deeply-held conviction by most people. It is the cause of much irritation in times of crises in public health when demands are made of scientists to provide the 'right' answer. From where did this notion arise? I have no ready answer but I know that those of us involved in science education have not done enough to get rid of it. We have taught our science courses, certainly over the years of compulsory education, as if exactness of measurement were an achievable reality. Some of us salved our consciences, but never bothered to illuminate our pupils, by occasionally muttering unconnected nonsenses such as 'due to experimental error' or 'to three significant figures' or 'if it's over halfway, round it up'. What is the history of these damaging traditions?

In my own case, it was a severe intellectual shock to me when I embarked on an Advanced-level course in physics to find that my measurements, which for five years had been spot-on or exact, were now deemed to be subject to errors and uncertainties. Even then, however, the new treatment was largely one of mathematics (complicated or 'fiddly', depending on your view); it was not a treatment that opened up my eyes to the nature of all knowledge gained through experimentation. My physics graphs were always straight and rarely missed the origin. Gradually, I came to understand, but what of my contemporaries who had ceased all contact with sciences at 16+? By the way, I would ban the origin from all graphs for the early stages of children's analyses. The reason would be to force all users of graphs (or should we call them 'readers'?) *firstly* to comment on the data that result from measurement, leaving until much later any thinking about the message that might be associated with a 'point' on the graph that was not and never could be measured.

Disappointingly for me, not much has changed since my own pupil days. Towards the end of my career, I was in conversation about his experiment with a very bright year 13 physics student, already Cambridge-bound. I was encouraged by his diligence, disappointed by his teacher's expectations and devastated by his evaluation of his investigation: *'Apart from the experimental error, this is a very good result'*. I hope his Cambridge experience set him right.

What is the remedy? How can we help pupils (society) to a better appreciation of data? We must be more honest and, from year 5? year 6?, assist pupils to acknowledge, discuss, estimate and record quantitatively the 'errors' in measurements. As a necessary corollary, we should never show 'points' on graphs, but regions defined by error bars. In this context, drawing lines of best fit (NC KS3, I'm pleased to note) will have meaning in *science* terms. If this happens (I am an optimist), we shall be more at ease with the uncertainties upon which our discipline so confidently rests.

Graphs should be viewed as works of art in that they portray behaviour. They convey messages. They are replete with suggestions for what might be happening in the system being studied. We are doomed if we see them only as sketches of data games. Let us heed the experience of Gladys, on her first journey by air. Excitedly settled in her seat and still enthralled by the wonder of it all, Gladys was not bothered when the Captain announced, *'The failure of one of our four engines means that our time of arrival will be delayed by two hours'*. Nevertheless, Gladys, who had been a diligent pupil in her Sc1 lessons, instinctively got out her writing pad and quickly sketched two axes on her graph, one axis for 'Number of engines failed' and one for 'Delay in flight'. Two further, precisely similar announcements followed. The outcome for Gladys was three 'points' on her graph. She noticed that the other passengers seemed to have other concerns, but she attributed this to their not having had such a rigorous training in data plotting. By way of easing their tension, she commented, *'I hope that the fourth engine does not fail because according to my graph, we could then be up here for a very long time.'*

Local customs

Arriving in Belfast, en route to Omagh for a primary science workshop, I puffed into customs with a small but barely portable trunk full of primary science equipment and materials. Every cubic centimetre had been made use of and I had breathed a sigh of relief on managing to close the clasps and turn the lock before leaving London.

The young, expressionless customs officer looked up at me, looked back at the trunk and said, *'Would you open it up, please?'* The first things to spill out, as the lid swung back, were some crocodile clips and leads. The officer's eyes fixed on the batteries beneath them. He stiffened. *'Would you unpack this case, please?'* he said. My heart sank. It had taken me hours to get everything in and I wasn't at all sure I could repeat this miracle of packing in the middle of a busy airport.

The first things to come out were a dozen used Nescafe coffee tins. *'What are these for?'* he asked. I felt he wasn't going to believe me as my disembodied voice said weakly, *'You tumble them about and guess what is inside by the sound and the feel.'*

'Would you open them up please, sir?' There was an emphasis on the 'sir' that boded ill. The first tin contained a ping-pong ball, the second some sand.

'Sand?' he said quizzically, stirring a finger in it. It was on the tip of my tongue to say, *'no, gunpowder'*, but the solemnity of the occasion coupled with better sense prevailed. By the time I had opened all twelve tins and explained their contents, a small crowd had gathered.

Never one to miss an educational opportunity and growing bolder, I drew the bystanders in to explain the intricacy of a tin-can telephone, how to blend colours by spinning tops and construct an arch from blocks of polystyrene. Cotton-reel tanks proved popular. A tin can that was rolled across the airport, only to suddenly return when everyone thought it had stopped, drew a round of applause.

We must have been at it for twenty minutes. In fairness to the customs officer, he mellowed as time passed and was kind enough to assist me with the re-packing. As the lid finally closed on the trunk he could contain his curiosity no longer. *'Are you anything to do with* The Generation Game?' he asked. I nodded my acquiescence.

Roy Richards

14 Chairing the Primary Science Committee in changing times

Anne Watkinson

Primary concerns become an established part of ASE business as it enters the 90s

Anne Watkinson trained in pathology and worked as a research assistant at Addenbrookes in Cambridge, doing cancer research. Later, marriage and children led her to become a playgroup leader and then regional organiser for the Pre-school Playgroups Association in Suffolk. Fascination with young children's learning persuaded her to train as a teacher and she taught in nursery and primary schools. She became a science co-ordinator, a headteacher, an LEA consultant, a senior schools adviser and even an Ofsted inspector, fighting consistently for good science education and for support for teachers. She chaired the ASE Primary Committee for several years. She has been outspoken in advocating the value and needs of teaching assistants (TAs), and is currently designing and writing induction materials for TAs for the DfEE, as well as writing two books and a PhD dissertation. In her 'spare time' she supports her children and six grandchildren (including a school governor, a PTA chair, some doing SATs and others learning to read) and looking forward to 'real' retirement sometime in the future.

Jumping in at the deep end: the 1980s

It has been hard to write this, particularly with dates, as the memories merge. I even had to track back in diaries to try to find out when I was chair of the ASE Primary Committee! I found that the minutes of my last committee meeting were in the summer of 1996 so I must have started with the committee in the 1980s.

Previously, I had worked in Essex on the ASE regional committee; the little primary sub-committee we had there used to meet in Jack Gill's lounge in Chelmsford, where we planned local meetings. It was my friends and colleagues there who pushed me into standing for the national committee – what one does in mad moments!

I was a headteacher at that time, recently coming from another headship which had been interesting so far as the science we had developed was concerned, but traumatic in its administration. The school was closed in 1990 because of its inadequate site. I had been through staff action, the after-effects of the Education Reform Act of 1987, the onset of the National Curriculum, directed time and the beginnings of LMS. I needed something positive, with wider horizons, and the ASE Primary Committee seemed a good opportunity. I had seen Audrey Randall – in her role as a member of the National Curriculum Working Party – perform in Essex University during the consultation for the first version of the National Curriculum, and had been impressed with her style, her knowledge and the fact that 'real' headteachers were able to influence Government documents. I thought I might even get to hear her again.

What was I letting myself in for? Who would elect me? I was unknown to those voting at ASE Council level but, much to my surprise, I was elected. With much trepidation, I went to my first meeting at Hatfield HQ one November day. We met in the Collating Room and started to go through the agenda. Then the chair, Colin Smith, put aside the agenda and said he had to tell us of his recent experiences on the new National Curriculum Council. I drank it in. Here was a real person involved at national level, able to participate on behalf of real teachers and schools – not just a faceless bureaucratic civil servant or politician deciding on policy. I felt welcome and glad that I had joined the group.

There were subsequent vibrant, informative and visionary meetings and, over time, I learned enough from everyone to become the chair at a later date. They were busy years. We saw through the consultation and the revision of the first set of National Curriculum documentation and the Dearing review. We raised other issues: assessment and record-keeping, the problems of KS2, science in the early years and a vision of the future. Throughout, we fought to maintain science within the whole curriculum and, although its importance may have slipped latterly, science is still a core subject and 2001 is the Year of Science.

What really stands out amongst all the changes, documentation and reports, are the people I met and their commitment. There were the HQ staff – David, John and Mavis, Jane and Colette – unsung heroes and heroines who work within constraints of space and finance to support the teachers teaching science. The other members of the committee who gave up their time so willingly to further the cause of primary science: Audrey and Roy, Rosemary and Gwill – who died too early – Maddie who enlightened us about Scotland and Jenny who did the same for us about Wales, Anne (the current Chair), Peter (former Editor of *PSR*), Neil, Flick, Barry, Rosemary, Tony,

The Primary Committee at ASE HQ, November 1992. From left to right: Audrey Randall; Flick Titley; Roy Richards; Anne Watkinson; Jenny Begg; John Lawrence; Neil Burton; Anne Goldsworthy and Rosemary Feasey

Lynne, Richard, Juliet. The reader may not know them, but they came in spite of family traumas and promotions. Why is it so many people who already do so much take on a lot more? I once said that some people have their golf clubs to go to at the weekend and I had the ASE. I still miss the friendship and sense of purpose we all felt.

The writing weekends stick in my mind: arriving at the Comet Hotel in Hatfield on a Friday evening to meet a group of like-minded folk for a meal; then down to hard work, arguing, challenging, explaining, trying to crystallise our thoughts and hopes in language to be understood by both ASE members and Government departments. Here again, people and events are memorable, e.g. the two Bobs and Phil, and trying to explain the strange man in my bedroom:

A strange man in my bedroom ...

How do you explain to your husband that editing a book entails working on the floor of a hotel bedroom with a strange man all evening? Fortunately, my husband is familiar with the demands of the ASE and he is also a scientist, although not in education. Writing weekends for the ASE meant working wherever there was space – sometimes in conference rooms, sometimes at Hatfield, and sometimes in a hotel bedroom!

The *Primary science – a shared experience* file was that in more ways than the title suggests. It was to get the artwork right that I had to meet the designer when we both had spaces in our diaries and somewhere to spread out the papers – hence Friday evening in the Hatfield Comet Hotel.

How do you spend *your* Friday evenings?

(That 'strange man' was me, and I'm designing this book as well! *Colin*)

The Primary Committee was responsible for many ASE publications. Apart from the *shared experience* for schools to share the science they did in school with parents and governors, we contributed to Rosemary Sherrington's *ASE primary science teachers' handbook* and made history by collaborating with other core subject organisations to produce *The National Curriculum – Making it work for the primary school* and *Teacher assessment – Making it work for the primary school.*

Chairing the Primary Committee meant attending ASE Council and, in the early days, the Executive Committee. If I had thought my first meeting at Hatfield was daunting, meeting Council members with vast experience of schools and the ASE was even worse. I hardly dared speak; the protocols, as with any organisation, were obscure and the language sometimes mystifying. At that time the Primary Committee was relatively new in the ASE and was of little standing, and, of course, to the majority of secondary teachers, primary teachers did not count anyway. Nevertheless, individuals were encouraging; I gained confidence and, with the advent of the National Curriculum for science, primary schools had to be recognised and valued. Primary membership slowly rose and primary business became an established part of Council business. The real 'coming of age' happened when a primary member, Rosemary Feasey, became chair of the Association for 1999–2000.

Changing times

There was considerable change during my time with the committee: writing policies for ASE, altering the constitution of committees to take account of the primary membership, etc. There was the strong move to relate science to everyday life and technology. John Stringer was writing the SATIS (Science and Technology in Society) materials and we met with him and enthusiasts from the Royal Society, BP and Courtaulds. I was invited to Sanctuary Buildings to meet with Cliff Gould HMI (Science) and found him and his colleagues positive, professional listeners.

The climax of the year was, as for many members, the Annual Meeting of the ASE. We were determined to raise the profile of primary science among all members and so tried various strategies. We started the special 'Primary Lecture' and I had to chair august people such as: Neville Evans HMI; Jim Rose, Senior Ofsted Inspector and one of the authors of the 'three wise men' report; Jim Campbell from Warwick – known proponent of the whole curriculum; and, at my last meeting, the Chief HMI, Chris Woodhead. I recall that lecture especially:

The Inspector called ...

It was the 1996 ASE Annual Meeting at Reading, with the Primary Lecture due to start at 2 pm. We were all geared up. The Primary Committee and about 200 others had their questions ready plus a few verbal rotten tomatoes and bad eggs; David Moore (Chief Executive) and the Association Chair were on tenterhooks, pacing the floor, waiting for the speaker who had still not arrived at 1.55 pm. I had practised my introduction before the mirror in the hotel that morning.

In he walked with less than five minutes to go. His PA had his briefcase with his notes and set them out on the podium, ready for him. I introduced him,

---

although everyone knew who Chris Woodhead was, and ASE had Her Majesty's Chief Inspector in their grasp for a whole hour – or did they?

He spoke for 40 minutes and then offered to answer questions. He was so disarming and astute that he deflected all our questions, responding only *'That's a good point'*. The audience was reduced to stunned silence and I was left searching the tiers in the lecture theatre long before 3 pm for more challenges from our members.

After the lecture, he continued in his charming way for another 40 minutes with the Primary Committee and his staff, and then congratulated us on keeping his attention – he had only allowed us 20 minutes in his busy schedule.

Was this the highlight of my time as the Primary Committee chair? No – the highlight of it all was the constant hard work, the friendship and good humour of the committee over the six years of my tenure. I have plenty of good memories – snapshots of working parties, volunteers working to put together publications, packages, etc. to support members.

The Chief HMI is no longer in post, but the ASE and the Primary Committee are still going strong. I wonder ... will Ofsted still be going from strength to strength in 100 years time?

We have made it!

You may have gathered from the above that I am basically a shy person and so felt really privileged at being part of a team at ASE HQ and nationally. One Annual Meeting, this support gave me the courage to stand on a coffee table in the bar of a university and tell those assembled at the primary reception about the work of the committee. When my husband finally accompanied me to a couple of Annual Meetings (did he come to see with whom I had been spending all those weekends in hotels or did he come for the interesting programme?), and saw me doing this act, he was a bit taken aback. He is still coming with me next January, so he must have found other things to entertain him. We introduced primary receptions and 'drop-ins' to meet the committee, and made sure there was a range of interesting items for the primary teachers who attended the meeting. I finally knew we had arrived as a committee when I overheard a couple of secondary teachers complaining that the programme had too much primary content!

Now, the primary membership is so integral to the work of the ASE that many of these special events are no longer needed. That is real success. There is still some way to go, I suspect, in the hearts and minds of a few secondary folk, but most would no longer dare to say, as they used to, *'Don't worry about the NC or what you do in primary school science, we shall start them all at level 3.'* According to the SATs results and the media, primary science is a success story, but I still worry that what has been a success is the teaching to the test, the recall of science facts. I do not doubt that the process/content debate will continue. We cannot have process without content and maybe we have the levels of content about right? The confidence of primary teachers in understanding science content is higher than it has ever been, but are children leaving year 6 really able to investigate, reflect, question, work collaboratively and challenge?

I thank the ASE and send a message to the Primary Committee: '*Carry on helping primary teachers to teach real science – both content and process. The recent publications prove how much you are doing to keep these flags flying – and you might spare a thought also for all the classroom assistants who help teachers to teach science.*'

15 The crab that would not wink ∽

Gerald Smith

Developing teachers'
and children's
knowledge and
confidence in the
physical sciences,
1970s–1990s

Gerald Smith taught in schools and colleges for 18 years before
joining the Middlesex University (formerly Polytechnic) where he
became Principal Lecturer and Director of the Science and Technology
Education Centre, the local SATRO (Science and Technology Regional
Organisation). He was a regular consultant to the Department of Trade
and Industry and chaired the DTI Working Party on Primary Science and
Technology. Gerald was a Member of the SCSST (Standing Conference
on Schools' Science and Technology) and was a frequent exhibitor and
spokesperson at national exhibitions and conferences. He had a
formative influence on the teaching and learning of electricity in
primary and secondary schools, publishing widely on this subject and
designing (with support) the widely successful *5–13 Electricity* kits.

T he early teaching schemes such as Nuffield Junior Science and Science 5/13
did not make the expected significant impact on schools, especially in the
physical sciences. Massive in-service efforts helped but not in every classroom of the 20,000+ primary schools in the country. Sets of published workcards
supplied some teachers with the background for science topics. Others got science
going by handing out workcards to pupils, each applied to a different topic and

What do they understand about electricity?

each with its own tray of equipment.

Lack of background knowledge and understanding, as well as poor self-confidence, were only overcome by long in-service courses. Very few teachers were able to benefit from such courses, even after the introduction of the '20 day' courses. The successful few often quickly became advisers, deputy heads, heads and lecturers (generally leaving the classrooms).

Some light was shed on the underlying problem of lack of confidence by the publications of Ros Driver and others in the mid-1980s. The retention of so-called 'misconceptions' of fundamental ideas in science went a long way towards explaining 'lack of confidence' in the primary teachers. In Middlesex, we decided to test every student entering teacher training over a five-year period. We discovered that a large percentage of each group held well-known misconceptions about electricity. Similar tests were given to groups of teachers, advisers and HMI at the ASE Annual Meetings and at one SATRO Leaders' Conference, with similar results. The one really sad result from these tests was that many of the delegates would not hand in their papers for checking!

Misconceptions in electricity were or are a particular problem. Even after quite an intensive practical course, older pupils revert to their former thinking, as was shown by Cosgrove in New Zealand. Research at Perth University showed that qualified electrical engineers can have a range of quite different views on 'how electricity works'.

Without any practical experience in electricity, misconceptions occur quite naturally. Without repeated practical experience, it is not possible to challenge and develop children's ideas. If we are to prepare children to live in an increasingly technological age, it is of fundamental importance that practical experiences in electricity should start in the nursery and infant school and continue all through the primary phase.

The development of the *5–13 Electricity* kits

I was determined to do what I could to inspire teachers and children with the same enthusiasm that I felt about electricity (and technology). I was in an ideal situation to do this as the leader of a SATRO, a lecturer and an in-service training provider.

I had attended an HMI course in 1965 directed by Len Ennever, and came away with a battery holder, bulb holder and switch mounted on 2 x 1 inch wood. The batteries were held in place by Terry clips and connections made between jug hooks, at the end of each block of wood, with crocodile clips. This was not perfect but a big improvement on the DIY paper-clips and drawing pins.

Back at the university, teachers and students on initial and in-service courses made hundreds of these 'electricity kits' under my supervision. But I kept asking myself, *'Why does primary science equipment have to be home-made?'* The lack of an existing well-made electricity kit on the market became a topic for discussion in the staffroom and at a number of SATRO working party meetings. My team and I accepted the challenge to produce a good, user-friendly electricity kit and, working with Barnet Teachers' Centre and classteachers across the region, the first prototypes were produced and tested in schools. As the local SATRO, we often sold packs of Perspex to local schools, so Perspex was therefore the obvious choice to replace wooden blocks. Even better, the packs were stored for us at the LEA Work Preparation Centre and they were willing to cut it into small pieces.

The best critics were the teachers and the children: they tried out the kits and then we modified them. When everyone was satisfied, the designs were approved and the first *5–13 Electricity* kits were sold to local schools.

Teachers and children were universally enthusiastic: the delight on children's faces when their bulbs lit up or their models worked was worth all the hard work. We knew from all the evidence that children learn to design most effectively if they are given lots of prior experience of making. This was the underlying philosophy of *5–13 Electricity*.

With the introduction of the National Curriculum for science, there was increased interest in the kits and requests for more materials. Chris Brantingham (a student with the Art and Design Faculty at Middlesex) explored the kit as part of her final-year work and designed the *Introduction and guide*, which has since gone out with thousands of kits around the country. In 1990, Chris and many local teachers helped us to design child-friendly workcards, *Make it work*.

The crab that would not wink

All this began to have an effect on the work done in primary electricity. In 1983, Standard Telephones and Cables were spending money to celebrate their centenary. We were helping them to spend some of their money by arranging an exhibition of work from local schools. The theme was 'New Technology' generally and 'Micro-electronics' in particular. To be honest, in 1983, there was not a lot of such work in schools, although our project 'Starting microelectronics' was by then being used by many of our local secondary schools.

After applying a lot of pressure, we persuaded quite a few primary schools to exhibit work that involved electricity. On the day, there was a good turnout of visitors from all aspects of education and quite a few from local industry. All seemed to be going very well. The SATRO staff were nodding and smiling confidently and mingling with the guests. Then there were was some disturbance from a group clustered around one of the exhibits. Angela, a local primary teacher from Barnet who had attended an in-service science course at Middlesex, was showing the group the Electric Crab that her class had made as part of a project on the seashore. The children had made a very large crab that moved sideways on a LEGO trolley. It had claws that could move to pinch a finger, eyes of different colours that would blink and wink and (with a little biological licence) a baby crab clinging to its back with the help of a magnet.

Unfortunately, ten minutes after the exhibition opened, the eyes stopped winking and blinking! The visitors, mainly from industry, were not content with smiling sympathetically and moving on. Their screwdrivers were out and the electrical connections were being investigated – a real example of partnership between schools and industry.

Changes in the 1990s

With the increasing emphasis on literacy and numeracy, it became more and more difficult to recruit teachers for science INSET. In 1991, once again with teachers' help, we published a self-teaching package, *Understand electricity*. However, distance learning is difficult when teachers have such heavy demands on their time. So are we making progress in the teaching of science?

• Long in-service practical courses are now a thing of the past.
• Evidence from the lack of sale of science equipment to primary schools indicates that, at the moment, science does not have a high priority.
• Most people agree that science should be a practical experience but there is less and less time for practical studies.
• The SATs at KS2 in science are supposed to gauge the children's knowledge and understanding – but do they simply involve using pencil-and-paper tests to assess the children's ability to acquire facts? Pencil-and-paper tests in science can disadvantage all children but particularly children with special educational needs.

I console myself with remembering what a pleasure and a privilege it has been to work with so many teachers and others in developing knowledge and confidence in electricity. If you use electrical kits with your children, remember that somewhere in a classroom cupboard, there is a dusty, blinking crab, waiting to return to life!

5–13 Electricity kits and materials are available from:

Training in Technology Ltd, Science and Technology Centre, Devonshire Hill School, Weir Hall Road, London N17 8LB. Tel. 020 8880 9972; Fax. 020 8386 2514.

Assessing children's learning in science: Electricity

What do these 5-year-old children know about electricity?

Electricity goes through metals better than cloth.

I don't know [what makes a television work].

You press that button and it comes on.

? [child shrugs].

Even if you've got a switch it won't work, 'cos you haven't got any batteries.

The electricity comes from the lightning in the sky.

[Silence – the child simply stares at the teacher]

The electricity comes into the school through wires under the ground and in the wall. It's joined up to those ... plugs ... in the wall ... with three holes in them.

Electricity is the same kind of thing as petrol – it makes things work.

You can make electricity do different things – like a light and a heater, and a magnet that picks up the cars in the junk yard.

I think it comes from water somehow but I don't know how.

There's a man in the sky – that one with the beard – he's got electricity in his body and he just touches the wires and makes electricity come in.

Transcripts from reception children; research by Max de Bóo

Transcripts from the SPACE research

These responses show how children are attempting to make sense of the varied sources of information and observations to which they are exposed:

Kelly Ann (age 9): I think electricity gets here by satellite.

Sonia (age 8): Electricity comes from God.

Interviewer: How does it get here?

Sonia: God brings it and puts it in those big round things [points to nearby gasometers].

Interviewer: How does he do that without us seeing?

Sonia: He made the round things before he made people and he put electricity in them.

Robert (age 10): It must go very fast ... faster than Concorde because you can phone to France in about 10 seconds, so electricity can get to France that quickly.

16 Reminiscences of advisory teachers ∽

Chris Macro

> ESG advisory teachers spread good practice in the mid-1980s

Chris Macro was a primary teacher for 20 years and then spent five years as an advisory teacher for science and technology with St Helens LEA. She was seconded to Liverpool University where she worked on a teacher education project with Wynne Harlen. Since 1990, she has been Senior Lecturer in Primary Science at Edge Hill College of Higher Education, contributing to initial teacher education programmes and involved in professional development for practising teachers. She has written articles for journals, is a co-author of children's science books and contributor to science teacher education books.

With thanks to **Karen Hartley**, former Advisory Teacher for Science with Knowsley LEA, for her additional 'memories'.

EDITORS' NOTE

One of the biggest influences on the improvement in primary science teaching and learning occurred when Government funding was found for science from the Education Support Grants (ESG) in 1985. Throughout the country, some of the best class teachers were brought out of their class-rooms to act as good role models and offer peer support to their colleagues in local schools. This was innovative and revolutionary – it had never been done before. Those who became advisory teachers for science (or science and technology) were chosen principally because they were good all-round class teachers, as well as inspirational in teaching primary science. That was what gave them credibility with their colleagues – not whether they had degrees in science (most of them did not). Chris Macro was one such. The positive impact that she and the other ATs had then (most funding was withdrawn in 1988), has left its legacy even to this day.

When, in 1986, the Senior Adviser of my Local Education Authority came to me and said, *'I'm here to offer you the position of advisory teacher for science and technology'*, my first reaction was one of pleasure. After all, I enjoyed teaching those subjects and I would be happy to spend all day doing just that. It was only later, when I began to think about exactly what the job entailed, that I began to be nervous. I didn't have a science degree; my experience was as a classroom teacher and I'd have to leave the school where I had been so happy for so many years. To compound the issue I was about to become the co-ordinator and leader of a team of one and I alone was responsible for strategic planning! Did I know enough to provide the required support?

I was fortunate to have colleagues in the teachers' centre who had been advisory teachers for maths and science. They had been in post for a year and were a great help to me in my planning. Even so, we felt rather isolated so we formed a self-help group with other advisory teachers from Merseyside and North Wales and occasionally met others in the North West to share experiences and training. Similar groups were getting together, such as that in Greater Manchester, set up by Stuart Naylor at Manchester Metropolitan University. Wynne Harlen, newly appointed as Professor of Education at Liverpool University, provided some training for our group and she inspired us all. I soon began an MEd degree with Wynne and this too increased my confidence. The IPSE (Initiatives in Primary Science Education) team – John Slade, Joy Wilson and Peter Petrie – appointed to evaluate the ESG projects, helped us by sharing strategies and success from groups around the country.

It was a privilege to work in so many classrooms and I'm sure that others would agree that we all learned a great deal from the teachers and children with whom we were working. We were very much feeling our way, making mistakes but achieving successes too. There were several amusing moments. I designed a project on electricity whereby I trained some sixth-formers in ten schools, who then worked in primary classes to support the children's learning about electricity. During one of my visits on these occasions, a child said with surprise, *'Oh, I didn't know you were a teacher. I thought you were an electrician!'*

Another advisory teacher, working on the theme of senses, had what he thought was a very good idea. In order to test the children's sense of smell, he took a child secretly into the stock room and sprayed perfume on to her skin. The child then mingled with the other children who had to identify which child was wearing perfume – a problem which they solved easily! Unfortunately, the story told by the (enthusiastic) child to her parents when she went home was that she *'was taken into the stock room by a man'*! Fortunately the irate parents were mollified when they heard the story next day – and the advisory teacher had learned a lesson too!

Yet another advisory teacher returned to a school where, two weeks earlier, she had helped the teacher to set up a 'touch table'. She was surprised to find the table in pristine condition. When she remarked on this, the teacher said, *'Oh, well, I didn't allow the children to touch anything. I didn't want it to get messed up.'*

Nevertheless, the message about scientific enquiries began to get through. The same advisory teacher was involved with an annual science fair, an interactive occasion in which teachers set up activities with children and adults. A local authority official approached a stand where some reception children were working with snails. He asked the teacher a question about the snails but before the teacher could answer a child said, '*Oh, no. We can't tell you that. What do you think?*' It was clear that these children were used to having their ideas valued.

The delight of children's ideas

The children's ideas were a revelation to me. After one in-service course, where we had explored the effects of compressed air by standing on a PE mat placed over some inflated balloons, one teacher went back to school and used an upturned table to show his children a similar effect. The following day, a year 2 child brought in a beautifully written account of how she had tried this at home with her parents and the budgie in his cage. She ended her writing by saying, '*I thought it was magic but my teacher said it wasn't magic. It was science.*'

I remember too, when I was working with some year 1 children who had been reading the story *Alfie's feet* (Shirley Hughes). We all took off our socks and shoes and examined our feet very carefully. The undersides of the children's feet were soft and pink, whilst mine were, to say the least, rather gnarled and calloused. '*Yours are different from ours*', said the children, and one child remarked, '*Your feet are very old and you've walked on them for years and years and years.*'

Looking back, I often wonder why we all enjoyed our work as advisory teachers so much. We worked very long hours, drove many miles in all weathers and spent a great deal of time simply loading and unloading resources from our cars. One advisory teacher became known as 'The Bag Lady'. Even so, I have never met anyone who did not enjoy the work. I think it was because every day was different. There was no time to be bored and the children were always at their best when learning science and technology – stimulating and exciting subjects for both teachers and learners. The teachers too showed interest and enthusiasm; many became firm friends during and long after my four years as an advisory teacher.

The friendship of other advisory teachers was also important to us. We met every year at the ASE Annual Meetings and also when we initiated advisory teachers' conferences. There are strong memories from those occasions, such as the technology sessions with David Jinks, seeing the science in making pancakes with Rosemary Feasey, dramatising science with Max de Bóo and hearing Karen Hartley, Kevin Cooney and Joan Boden explain the SPACE research being carried out at that time (Science Processes and Concept Exploration).

Most of us are still in science education: we look a little older but we still retain our enthusiasm and feel that our lives and careers have been greatly enriched by our experiences as advisory teachers.

Overheard on a visit to a primary school:

World-weary, male, very experienced headteacher: *You are most welcome. Come and go as and when you please, work with whoever you choose – in whatever way you decide. You don't need to bother asking my permission.*

Young, enthusiastic, female IPSE advisory teacher: *But I want you to be bothered. I want you to be actively involved, knowing what I am doing – and evaluating my effectiveness.*

John Slade

Director of the IPSE team (Initiatives in Primary Science Education) monitoring and evaluating the effectiveness of the ESG (Education Support Grant) Initiative

---

113

The diary of an ESG Advisory Teacher, 1985

September – Monday 2nd: First day in ESG Primary Science! Given room full of laboratory equipment in an empty building vacated by the secondary school next door. A left-over smell of gas, or something else? Telephone not working. Must buy solvent for removing bubble-gum from clothes.

Wednesday 4th: In-service course. Informed about the ASE, the JISST, BAYS and the SRAT* Must remember the mnemonic for multiple acronyms (or is that an unpleasant disease?).

Monday 9th: No keys for our new room. Worked in the corridor. Telephone not working anyway.

Thursday 12th: Got some keys. Found a toilet in the building that nearly flushes. Telephone engineer coming tomorrow!!

Friday 13th: Telephone engineer came. Cut us OFF!

Monday 16th: Borough engineer came to look at the lab. equipment. Said he'd have to bring the Borough architect to look at the problem.

Friday 27th: Fed up with our name – no-one knows what ESG stands for. So far we have been called the ECG, the ENT and the EEC. The next person to get it wrong will get my version of ECT – Electro-Convulsive Therapy!

PS. After a therapeutic lunchtime in the Bricklayers Arms, we've settled on Primary In-Service Science Educational Developers – nice initials!

October – Monday 6th: The Borough engineer brought the Borough architect to look at the laboratory equipment. He said he will bring someone from the Education Committee to look at it.

Thursday 9th: Back in schools again but suffering from an identity crisis – the first teacher asked if I was a student, the second if I was a parent!

November – Friday 22nd: Car problems. Left the lights on outside school – flat battery. AA busy but came at last. AA man wasn't exactly rude about the age of my Mini – just told me how much he admired me for continuing to drive it!

December – Monday 1st: Tried to find a room for a teachers' in-service course. The first floor has electric light and water but no heating. The second floor has heating and light but no water. The only room that has all three is the caretaker's little room underneath the boiler house. Could we ask the teachers to ...? Oh, well. Just a thought.

Christmas Convalescence Period: Wrote a checklist for all new, unsuspecting ESG Advisory Teachers:

ON PLACING A FACE

• Faces less than one metre from the ground can usually be considered to belong to children. (No adult with any sense would abase themselves in front of advisory teachers.)

• A face considerably higher than one metre from the ground could belong to one of the following groups: (a) a teacher, (b) a headteacher, (c) another ESG teacher, (d) your science adviser. Take care at this stage; these groups are difficult to distinguish – all look harassed and underpaid!

• If you are greeted, you are likely to be in the presence of a teacher or headteacher. Clearly you are memorable, although it is not always clear for what. You will usually recognise a teacher whose class you have encountered at close quarters – shared experience of this sort makes for something closer than acquaintance!

• If, when you meet, the person changes direction to walk with you and effortlessly includes passing strangers in the conversation, you are probably listening to a headteacher. This group has developed an ability to hold ad hoc, miniature, peripatetic staff meetings that last as long as it takes to get from a classroom to the staffroom. If, as the person talks, s/he suddenly develops a limp or in any other way slows the pace, you are definitely listening to a headteacher.

• Conversations starting with, *'Have you a room/telephone?'*, *'When are you moving to new premises?'* are all opening gambits of other ESG teachers. It is necessary to decide fairly quickly whether you say that everything is fine or tell the truth from the start.

• If you experience an uncontrollable urge to say things beginning, *'Could you tell me ...?'*, *'How can I ...?'* or *'When will they ...?'* then you are talking to your science adviser.

• In all the above situations, the effort needed to remember the name that goes with the face will detract from the concentration necessary to preserve even a passing resemblance to an air of competence.

• If you still cannot place the face, it will probably belong to a member of your family.

Max de Boo

*SRAT: Senior Ratcatcher at Twickenham

17 From the East End to early years and the ASE

Max de Bóo

> How a reluctant recruit to the profession ended up in the thick of of it

Max de Bóo taught science and mathematics in secondary schools in the UK and Argentina. After her family circumstances changed (a mother of two children, and later a lone parent), she worked as a child-minder, a nursery teacher and manager, and taught in infant and junior schools. She always specialised in science and maths/IT, although she spent a lot of time as the only school pianist/concert organiser/'theatrical' director too. She became an advisory teacher for science in Haringey, working with teachers from nursery through to year 6, spent two years in research, and ten years lecturing on primary science and technology in three universities and in national and international in-service courses. She has published many articles and books on science education and early-years education.

My beginnings

My primary schooling took place just after the Second World War in the 1940s. We had left London after the Blitz and gone to live in the country. I was lucky in many ways: although wartime deprivation meant limitations on food and clothing, my education was in safe hands. My playgrounds were the fields, the hedgerows and the woods. My mother would drag us out on cold nights to *'come and look at the stars'*. I learnt so much and was lucky to have some primary teachers who were enthusiastic and flexible, practical and approachable. We regularly went out to the local woods to explore, observe, draw – and turn our experiences into drama. When we left the country for the town again, secondary education turned out to be a shock – didactic and prescriptive.

As a result, I never intended to teach. When I was at secondary school in the 1950s, most girls were not expected to 'have a career', so gaining qualifications was less important. There was no career guidance for the girls in my school. Apart from five great teachers in my secondary school (three science, one English and one maths), there were appalling teachers and rampant bullying. I truanted frequently (regular visits from the truant officer) and found myself at 18 years with limited qualifications. After a year doing manual jobs (waitress, YMCA cook, hotel cleaner, etc.), I went reluctantly to teacher training college whilst I thought about what I really wanted to do.

How I got into college is still a mystery – when the Deputy Principal asked me at the interview 'as a chemist' which toothpaste to use, I told her to scrape off the soot from the back of the chimney, mix it with soap and scour her teeth with that. Did this woman recognise the potential teacher in me or were they just as desperate for recruits to the profession as they are now?

Even armed with a teacher's certificate, I did not want to teach but my research into junior company executive jobs revealed gross inequalities in treatment and attitudes towards male and female employees. By the time I went down to London to find a teaching post, the only vacancy left was as a secondary science teacher in the East End of London in what was locally known as the 'dustbin' school of Hackney.

Baptism of fire

That was a grim year. The East End of London had been badly hit in the Second World War and, although this was 20 years later, very little reconstruction had taken place. Locals lived in houses shored up by planks or in cheap tenements. The old three-storey Victorian school building stood beside a factory, both surrounded by an enormous, undisturbed bomb site. This environment had its effect on the people and children living there. Families lived on very low wages, on 'the welfare' or on crime. My first morning as a teacher was salutary. I was standing nervously in my classroom waiting for the incoming first-year pupils when in came the Deputy Head, knee-high to a grasshopper but with a backbone of reinforced steel. She asked me, *'Do you know where to hit them so it doesn't bruise?'* I didn't, so she showed me by hitting me hard – it hurt but it didn't bruise!

However, I was one of a newer breed of teachers and could not bring myself to use that sanction. I tried goodwill instead but lacked experience or authority. In the event, I learned to cope with abuse – verbal and physical – and theft of my possessions and cash (devastating on a probationer's pay).

I tried to teach science but with limited success. For example, I had to teach human biology to 15-year-old girls who were (almost) all 'on the game'. Each day a crop of girls was brought in by the police who had found them soliciting in the local park. These girls knew more than me about the facts of life – they collapsed in hysterical laughter at my attempts at sex education!

On another occasion, my colleague and I asked the first years (11–12 year-olds) to bring in pieces of fruit – to draw in her art class and then investigate in science. To

Investigating bubbles in the nursery (Acresfield Nursery School, Middleton, Manchester)

our enormous surprise, all the pupils arrived with a piece of fruit that morning, followed 20 minutes later by an irate barrow boy from the street market.

The year was grim but the support and laughter in the staffroom was unforgettable.

The following four years included a dreadful year teaching on Tyneside, two years teaching in Buenos Aires and another year teaching juniors in London. It was only when I took maternity leave and started reflecting at home that I realised with surprise that I had fallen into the best job in the world with the best specialism. Like someone who has just avoided an accident, I could hardly think about what might have happened if I hadn't become a teacher. All the awful experiences could not diminish my enthusiasm and determination to open children's eyes to the wonders and delights of the world.

Getting hooked on primary education

Subsequent years as a single parent (1970s and early 1980s) gave me an insight into attitudes and prejudices towards women, single parents and education phases. I had to take any teaching jobs I could get and still support my children. I did child-minding, taught in and managed a nursery for three years, taught junior children and infants and did private tuition (evenings and weekends). I was accorded less respect by former secondary colleagues as a primary teacher and even less when I worked with nursery children. Many people asked me *'When are you going back to real teaching in secondary school?'*

Nevertheless, I was fascinated by young children's development and their responses to practical primary science. I was filled with missionary zeal for science and education in the early years. I took curriculum responsibilities for maths, IT and science. I was lucky in that the education world was also changing then. UNESCO and later the UK Government published documents describing the entitlement of children to science education (e.g. *Science 5–16: a statement of policy*, DES, 1988).

There were opportunities for distance learning (Open University) a part-time diploma and other courses, ideal for adults with dependants. I took advantage of everything. SATROs (Science and Technology Regional Organisations) were having greater influence and ASE was finally beginning to recruit primary members.

The ESG initiative and advisory teaching

Money was being found to promote children's science education. Government initiated 'Education Support Grants' (ESG) across England and Wales. Local education authorities who applied for the funding submitted plans for recruiting and training advisory teachers who would support primary teachers in their teaching of science. Team sizes varied from 3 or 4 people to single individuals but the idea was that *experienced primary classroom teachers* should play a major role in helping their colleagues in local schools. Strategies for this varied from programmes of INSET in the new teachers' centres to team-teaching in the classroom.

I became an advisory teacher in Haringey under the enlightened leadership of Jim Ritchie (Science Adviser) who adopted, modified and implemented all the best practice from the innovative work done by the, then disbanded, Inner London Education Authority (ILEA) science teams. It was fast-moving, exciting and successful: the funding enabled us to give the schools and individual teachers in-depth support. Most teachers responded to the initiative with enthusiasm and commitment, not an easy thing to do when 9 out of 10 teachers were afraid of science and had no confidence in their ability to teach it. Nevertheless, these highly professional teachers succeeded in improving their science teaching and this success story was echoed around the country.

The ESG advisory teachers (ATs) were an incredible bunch of experienced, dynamic, stimulating but often isolated experts. We met infrequently, so I started a newsletter (*Pri-Sci*) as another means of keeping in touch. We shared ideas, methodologies and anecdotes:

> Headteacher giving a class teacher a packet of Blu-tack: *Well, that's used up this year's science budget.*
>
> Class teacher, assuming that the advisory teacher was free supply cover: *Don't worry – I'll come into the classroom for a full half-hour later today.*
>
> Year 2 child, writing up her observation: *I saw a egog awtsld.* [I saw a hedgehog outside.]
>
> Copied from the wall in Southgate Underground Station: *Bad spellers of the world untie!*

One of the places where primary science enthusiasts met and swapped ideas was at the Annual Meeting of the ASE. In 1981, ASE was still dominated by male, secondary and tertiary members. At the Annual Meeting of 1982, there were only about 50 of us primary members (mostly female). We went to everything we could find but there was no choice on the programme. By the last day we were fed up with receiving the kind of advice and support we ourselves gave to new, inexperienced colleagues, and fed up with the lack of new ideas on policy and practice. The speaker on that last day, albeit innocent and well-intentioned, got it in the neck. We did everything but walk out: we argued, criticised, demanded, catcalled – and decided that we had to put on a programme for ourselves at the next Annual Meeting.

Which we did. Primary membership of the ASE in 2001 is now over 3000 and a substantial number of them, including groups from member primary schools, attend the Annual Meeting. There is greater choice of primary talks and workshops than ever before, although we always need more.

My work with the ASE

I seem to have spent a lot of time with the ASE. I was drawn to it originally in the late 1970s when I attended a local Section meeting on primary science. At the end I waited to complain about how little support the ASE gave to primary teachers. One by one, the members of the committee took me gently to task, explaining that they did as much as they could in the circumstances but needed more active primary members and would I like to be co-opted on to the committee? It was an introduction to the unsung host of people who work tirelessly and freely for the ASE in local Sections and Regions, promoting all that is best in science education.

I dived in at the deep end and, before long, was secretary and then chair of that Section, as well as a committee member on another Section later. I wrote materials and helped to organise conferences for the ASE. I joined the editorial board of *Primary Science Review*, becoming an assistant editor, and worked on other ASE committees, such as Publications, Research and the recent Initial Teacher Training group. Just like Anne Watkinson (Chapter 14), I can remember the hectic times when weekends were spent at ASE HQ. I also remember the hilarious return train journeys from *PSR* meetings in Liverpool, when Roy Richards and Audrey Randall regaled us with spicy anecdotes that cannot be repeated here!

Full circle?

History has a way of surprising us. In my last university, I spent five years training teachers, working in a science 'classroom' which had been a hospital ward for soldiers wounded at the front during the Second World War. After the war, this room and others in the Mansion House, were used to give a one-year crash course in teaching to replace the many teachers who had died in the war. I don't know how they did it, but I know I was taught by some of them – primary teachers who inspired and motivated me and gave me a taste for the delights of environmental science.

So, my enthusiasm for science education is undiminished. Whilst I may groan at the limitations on time and the narrow-minded views of less-informed politicians and the media, I know that there are excellent teachers still achieving the 'wow!' effect by teaching primary science practically and effectively.

There is still some way to go but we have come a long way. All children now study science and all primary teachers study science. We have yet to succeed in persuading all children of the relevance of science to their daily lives and to see themselves as critical guardians against the use and abuse of science and misinformation parcelled out by politicians and the media. Maybe this is the task for the teachers of the new century.

18 Primary science arrives

Rosemary Feasey

| Primary science becomes a statutory part of the curriculum in the 1990s and the ASE elects its first 'primary' chair

Rosemary Feasey is currently Programme Director for Initial Teacher Training at the University of Northumbria. She was Lecturer in Education at the University of Durham where she ran a number of successful research and curriculum development projects on investigative science, effective questioning, literacy in science, numeracy in science and key skills. She has written extensively in primary science and is part of the GINN Star Science writing team. Formerly a deputy head and advisory teacher for science, she has remained close to the classroom throughout her career and regularly provides science in-service work both at national and international level. Rosemary was the first person from a primary education background to be elected as Chair of the Association for Science Education in its 98-year history.

My background

Reflections are such a personal thing; we all look at the same scene through different-coloured spectacles, which are tinted by our own experiences. When I look at the development of primary science over the last 25 years, I see my own career which developed almost simultaneously with the growth of science teaching in schools. I was a product of the education in the 1960s, but missed the so-called progressive teaching, since I attended a rural school where there were only four children in my year 4 class. It was cosy and we worked towards the 11+ exam but science was no more than nature study, which at best was a few twigs and conkers on a table and at worst the annual revisit to the frog life-cycle.

Science almost passed me by until I started teaching and was faced with a difficult class of 7 and 8 year-olds. They were the class that reduced me to tears when, as 10 and 11 year-olds, I was given them for a second time. They were a 'challenging' group of children until I discovered that practical hands-on science was the subject that they enjoyed – they released so much interest and creativity. Today I sometimes meet those children, now successful adults, and they tell me how much they enjoyed being in my class, especially when they had science!

Success for the children and myself kindled inside me a desire to develop further my own science knowledge and understanding, and, as a result, my own teaching. Gradually, I joined a small band of people within my local authority who had some expertise in this emerging curriculum area. My new-found expertise prompted me to apply for curriculum leader posts for science in schools, although as a shy young teacher I had a lot to learn. My first interview, which resulted in being appointed as curriculum co-ordinator for science, opened my eyes to a range of prejudices that I had not, until this point, encountered. It was the early 1980s and a very male-dominated local authority; I was the only woman to be interviewed. I learned after the interview that one of the other candidates had commented, *'A bloody woman got it, and a slip of a thing at that!'*

After that I gained confidence to move around different schools and, like other people involved in primary science at that stage, was appointed to one of the many science advisory teams around England and Wales, funded by Government Education Support Grants. Interestingly, in Durham our advisory team consisted of four women and one man, which seemed to astound the then Director for Education until it was pointed out that the make-up of the team was roughly the ratio of women to men in teaching.

The response to science advisory teachers

Prejudice against primary science and women took many forms and was often subtle but at other times quite overt. I was frequently challenged by a small minority of teachers for whom science was a pernicious threat and to be avoided at all costs. Sometimes, their fear was based on their own lack of confidence; this was particularly so with women teachers who had experienced almost no science in their own education. Other people felt threatened because I was relatively young or because I was a woman. Some men did not take kindly to a woman in a science advisory role and occasionally female teachers by-passed me and headed straight for the only male colleague on the team, thinking that he was more knowledgeable and, because he was a man, must be the leader.

Happily, although such prejudice showed in a significant minority of teachers, the majority were eager to explore this new curriculum area. My enthusiasm and expertise grew as an advisory teacher. I learned a great deal from others in advisory roles, from teachers in schools and most of all from the children. Like many of my colleagues, I was called the 'science person' or 'science lady' and was often overwhelmed by the enthusiasm and hunger of young children to explore and find out.

The 1980s was a period of huge growth in primary science, supported by government money and intervention. We felt like pioneers, which looking back we were. The mould was broken in so many ways: science into primary schools, women teachers engaging in science, children questioning and taking part in hands-on activities, and teachers gradually breaking down their own fear of science.

Changes in initial teacher training

Most science advisory teachers had a short shelf-life, and like many of my colleagues I did not return to teach in the classroom but chose to teach primary science on initial teacher training courses. The influx of primary women – and men – advisory teachers into higher education totally changed the face of initial teacher training. At this point (1989), the Government also changed the status of primary science on initial teacher training courses, from being an optional couple of hours to being a compulsory core subject which was afforded 150 hours of time. Suddenly, every student came through my hands and I realised the enormity of the responsibility. The introduction of the National Curriculum provided me with the backdrop for in-service and curriculum publications, plus opportunities for working at national level. Here I had the best of all worlds. Like a schoolgirl in a sweetie shop, I was hungry for everything the role offered and greedily involved myself in as much as possible.

Over the years, this has resulted in opportunities to work with hundreds of established teachers and students and I have never ceased to be amazed by their capacity for hard work and willingness to develop new ideas and approaches to teaching science. To be part of helping a teacher change from someone who is nervous and sceptical about science in the primary classroom, into a confident, enthusiastic teacher, is the most rewarding part of my job. Recently, a student sat talking to me about an impending Ofsted visit. She was due to be observed and interviewed on her final school practice, as part of an inspection of the English component of the ITT course. At the beginning of the course, she, like many other students, did not particularly like science, having had an indifferent experience at secondary school. I smiled as she said, *'I wish they were coming to see me teach science instead of English. I love teaching science, that's where my best lessons are and the kids really behave and have a great time. I'd really show Ofsted then!'*

The advent of the National Curriculum

At my interview for the post of primary science lecturer I was asked to suggest whether the introduction of a National Curriculum would be a good thing or not. My response was, *'I have no idea. Do you?'* It seems rather stupid now: I can only think that they were impressed by my audacity to turn the question back on to them, since they gave me the job.

Today, if you asked the same question, I would have to reply, *'Of course it's a good thing.'* The advent of the National Curriculum for England and Wales in 1989 (Scotland and Northern Ireland published their own curriculum documents shortly after) placed science firmly on the curriculum map. It provided the catalyst for massive in-service training in primary science, and produced an army of advisory teachers, many of whom are now the movers and shakers in education. More importantly, it gave children access to an extraordinary area of human endeavour, which is central to daily life. It has also increased the likelihood that the public will become more scientifically literate, challenge scientists, and engage in more democratic debate about how science should influence and mould life.

The ASE and my role as Chair

The role of subject associations in the development and support of primary science as a core subject in the primary curriculum must never be underestimated. Many of the changes in the curriculum have been as a direct result of the influence of the ASE. Those working within the Association have, over the years, helped to build up within various Government agencies a respect for ASE as the leading organisation in science education.

As the Government developed a National Curriculum and elevated science to a core subject, the primary membership of ASE grew and peaked during the early years of the National Curriculum. Such a sudden and large influx of a new group of people into ASE challenged many aspects of this large, traditionally secondary-dominated association. Many secondary members were hostile to primary and change has been slow, as is often the case in such large organisations, but today ASE has a thriving and well-respected group of primary members who work tirelessly to maintain the profile of primary science and improve primary practice. Alas, I am still dismayed to find many primary science co-ordinators are not members of their own subject association.

It was only a matter of time before someone from the primary ranks should take on the mantle of Chair of the Association. When I was asked, my decision to accept was not taken lightly. Taking on the role of the first Chair of ASE from a primary background was a huge responsibility. Of course, any Chair must represent all members, from students to secondary teachers through to technicians, to the best of his or her ability. However, there was undoubtedly the need to show ASE members, Government and representatives from other organisations, that a person from a primary background can be equal to (if not better than!) any other person, from whichever area of science. At the same time, there were expectations that the first Chair from a primary background would raise the profile of primary science and, on behalf of primary members, make the most of the position.

It was an enormous privilege to have the opportunity to be Chair of the ASE. It never failed to be challenging and sometimes the learning curve was vertical, especially when having to represent other sectors of science education, such as 11–16, post-16 and technicians, or trying to pin down a minister to agree to a course of action. It was though, without a doubt, the highlight of my career.

I began as a primary teacher, with no other ambition than to be good at my job and ended up as Chair of a national teachers' association. At the beginning, my career aspirations were non-existent. I saw myself as capable in the classroom but not with any real ability outside of that domain. I still don't have a career plan, so how did I end up here? I was once described as being 'quietly enthusiastic' about primary science and was upset not to be described as 'incredibly passionate about her subject'. Without realising it, over the years I had developed a personal mission, which even today remains central to my work. I simply want other people to share my enthusiasm and love for primary science and to help develop teachers' understanding and confidence. That is what has driven me in my career, and what led me to my role as Association Chair.

Concerns for the future

Enthusiasm is not everything – mine or other people's; we must be alert to many of the dangers that can befall a curriculum area. Already, there are signs that all is not well in primary science. Teachers admit to becoming less creative and more willing to follow national schemes and offer a minimalistic science, which is mundane for both children and teachers. Tests dominate the final years of primary education in England and Wales, and teaching and learning is compromised to ensure that national averages are reached and league tables are consistently good. Whilst understandable in a climate of accountability and inspection pressures, the result is that professional integrity in primary science is pared to the bone. Primary science has come a long way over the span of my own career but it has travelled that distance because of people who challenged the 'norm', stood up to authorities and showed through research how capable young children can be. They mixed passion for the subject with determination and a good dose of realism.

In the beginning, my main audience was teachers in the classroom and, of course, the children. Today that has changed; my audience remains teachers in the classroom and children but my passion is to take my missionary zeal to tomorrow's teachers, those in training and those yet to join the profession. Why? Because they are the people who will extend the boundaries of teaching science in the future. They are the ones for whom a national curriculum, Ofsted, and SATs will become the norm, and who will be able to make each of these fade into the distance, as background noise, to be listened to only when appropriate. But that will only happen if they are taught that they are the professionals and they can and must put these external pressures into perspective.

Only then can tomorrow's teachers get on with the real job – of teaching children and becoming the next generation of movers and shakers in science and potential Chairs of the Association for Science Education.

As a profession, we must not let the enthusiasm and the passion die. Future generations of children need teachers who are able to offer challenging and exciting primary science. More importantly, children need teachers who are prepared to explore those places into which primary science has not yet ventured. Government ministers and inspectors will not lead the way: we, the professionals in the classroom and in teacher education, are the people who will do that. Therefore, we must not discard the ownership of teaching and learning or the enthusiasm and passion for our subject.

19 Primary science: challenges for the future

Derek Bell

ASE's Chair in its centenary year reflects on the future of primary science

Derek Bell is Chair of the Association for Science Education for 2000–2001 and is currently Vice-Principal at Bishop Grosseteste College. He has over 20 years experience in teaching and teacher education. Throughout his career he has maintained a strong and active interest in the enhancement of teaching and learning, and approaches to helping children develop their understanding of the world around them. Derek was a member of the SPACE (Science Processes and Concept Exploration) Project team and acted as co-ordinator of the Nuffield Primary Science Project which developed from the SPACE work. Current research interests include children's understanding in science with particular reference to children with moderate learning difficulties, and the roles of subject leaders. He has published widely in primary science and is joint author of *Towards effective subject leadership in the primary school*, published by the Open University Press.

I was talking to some friends and colleagues at a recent ASE meeting and catching up with what they had been doing over the last few years. It didn't seem two minutes since they had been advisory teachers, working to help teachers to do science with their children before the National Curriculum had been introduced. Primary science has come a long way since then.

I know we all remember times slightly differently but no one can deny that the development of primary science has been a success. From its earliest beginnings, on through the projects of the 1960s and 1970s, to the incorporation of primary science as a core subject in the National Curriculum, science has provided an exciting and stimulating dimension to the curriculum for generations of primary school children and their teachers. If there is a theme flowing through the history of primary science then, I would suggest, it is the sense of enthusiasm, energy and enjoyment that has been generated by, and for, everyone involved. This is certainly something we must hang on to in the future despite the various pressures that face all of us involved in primary education.

Talking with those friends and colleagues started me thinking about the future of primary science and some of the big challenges we face. I hope that putting my thoughts on to paper might stimulate discussion and debate. My ideas are not comprehensive: there are many other things we might like to focus on but I have tried to outline the main areas we need to work on if we are to keep primary science going forward as successfully as it has so far.

We must remember, however, the rapidity of the changes that have taken place in the last ten years or so and the major impact these have had on primary schools generally as well as primary science in particular. The evolution of the National Curriculum, the associated assessment regime, the introduction of strategies to improve literacy and numeracy, and school inspections, among other things, have all influenced the way in which primary science has developed in the 1990s. While many of the positive features of primary science can still be found in classrooms throughout the country, we must add a note of caution and concern. The responsibilities and pressures which result from the status of science as a core subject and the 'league table mentality' which exists have resulted in many teachers, for good reason, shifting the focus of their teaching to emphasise the knowledge required by children to score highly in the tests. In short, there is danger of the primary science curriculum, as experienced by children, becoming content-laden and uninspiring, quite the opposite of what it should be. We must not ignore the alarm bells that this sets off but we should have every confidence that we have enough evidence and experience to take primary science into the future with even greater success. I have come up with four areas to which we need to give some attention.

Effective interactions between teachers and pupils

Although the pressures and constraints imposed by the external requirements and the day-to-day demands make life in the classroom difficult, it is ultimately the quality of the interactions between teachers and their pupils that is the key to the quality of the science learning that takes place. The tradition of enthusiastic teachers of science is a major asset but we know that it requires more than this to bring about effective teaching and learning in science. The improved levels of teachers' confidence in and understanding of science, and the increased use of approaches to teaching that are informed by knowledge of children's existing ideas, have helped to raise the overall standards in primary science. There is still work to be done, however, and we need to move on to identify ways in which the increased confidence, knowledge and understanding can be translated into more effective teaching, and hence learning, both inside and outside the classroom.

We can learn from what has happened in the National Literacy and Numeracy Strategies but, if the aim is to improve the teaching of primary science, then it is important to explore the issues involved in this specific domain. It seems to me that we need to look at what happens in science lessons and ask to what extent the children are fully engaged with the aspect of science being addressed. I'm not saying that children are not involved in doing the activity with enthusiasm and commitment, because in my experience they almost certainly will be. I am saying that for many children it doesn't get much beyond the 'doing' and so the quality of learning is somewhat superficial.

We need, therefore, to find ways in which the dialogue between the teacher and learner can be enhanced through, for example, the effective use of language and discussion as vehicles for the development of ideas. The language of science, however, is not simply the terminology of the different disciplines but it is also the threads, constructions, themes and stories of science which go together to explain what is understood to be science and the phenomena that are being investigated. The use of questions and the art of questioning by both the teacher and the learner are vital elements in developing the dialogue. Initially, this involves eliciting the learners' questions, then helping them to ask more appropriate questions and finally utilising their questions to bring about further investigation, discussion and thinking.

'Science for all'

My second point is related to the first in that we must make the phrase 'science for all' mean something in practice and ensure that the dialogue between teacher and learner, referred to above, includes all children. Under the National Curriculum, 'science for all' is a reality in the sense that science is a core subject and therefore it is for everyone up to the age of 16. In practice, however, this is not necessarily so. The latest version of the NC, introduced in September 2000, has in it a statutory statement on 'inclusion' which requires us to *provide effective learning opportunities for all*'. It goes on to set out three principles for ensuring this happens: setting suitable learning challenges; responding to pupils' diverse learning needs; and overcoming potential barriers to learning and assessment for individuals and groups of pupils. Each of these is easy to say but more difficult to achieve in practice.

We are, however, now much more aware of the needs of children with learning difficulties, those who are gifted and talented as well as those who have other special needs because of physical or behavioural problems. We are also much more sensitive to issues of gender, social, cultural and racial differences and therefore better able to respond to the needs of a wider range of pupils. The challenge is to translate our awareness into good practice in the learning environment, be it in the classroom or elsewhere. Above all, this requires all of us to recognise that the curriculum should not be used as a 'one size fits all' model, and that we adapt our teaching to match the needs of the children we are working with. In my own work I have found that there is a great deal of excellent practice which needs to be disseminated more widely so that many more children and teachers benefit.

Relationship between research and practice

The problem of dissemination brings me to the third area that I think we need to work on in order to ensure that the quality of teaching and learning in primary science continues to progress, and that is the relationship between research and practice. Almost everyone would accept that research should inform practice and indeed that practice should inform research. The SPACE (Science Processes and Concept Exploration) Project, which you remember was directed by Wynne Harlen at Liverpool University and Paul Black at King's College London, provided an excellent example of how research, curriculum development and classroom practice might be combined to bring about improved learning experiences. The influence of the project, which also produced the Nuffield Primary Science materials, has extended well beyond its official life-span and in turn given rise to much more work. One of the things that the SPACE Project did was to bring together three important ingredients for teaching and learning in primary science: the existing ideas which children bring to particular areas of science; the need to build on these ideas towards improved scientific understanding; and the importance of scientific processes in helping children to improve their understanding of the concepts. More recently, the AKSIS project, jointly undertaken by the ASE and King's College London (which includes Anne Goldsworthy, current Chair of the ASE Primary Committee in the team), is an excellent example of how detailed research and the subsequent development of practice can be used to improve teaching of particular aspects of science.

Clearly, research is important to underpin the curriculum development and to explore ways in which we can improve our practice. The challenge we face is to find ways of bringing researchers and teachers even closer together to work in partnership. It is only by strengthening the dialogue between the two that real progress will be made. Once again, we have made significant progress but there is still some way to go.

Science as part of everyday life and culture

The fourth issue is the need to recognise that science does not take place in a vacuum: it is part of everyday life and culture. While the majority of children may never actually use the science they learn directly, either personally or professionally, everyone will be faced with decisions that require some understanding of science. What have become classic examples in recent years – the debates on BSE and GM crops – involve everyone making personal decisions that may have an effect on them in the future. Science as part of everyone's education has an important role to play, not simply as part of the decision-making process, but also because it is part of what we are. Encouraging children to develop the ability to approach problems in a scientific manner helps prepare them for many aspects of their future life. The challenge we face throughout science education is finding ways to articulate this more clearly and incorporate it effectively into the curriculum. Science as a subject and a way of working provides us with opportunities that are only limited by what our imagination can conceive.

Continuing professional development

I realise that I have glossed over some of the practical problems that must be overcome in meeting the broad challenges that I have outlined, but I am confident that we can succeed. I am also convinced that one of the key elements is improvement in the quality of continuing professional development for everyone – teachers, researchers, managers, consultants, teaching assistants, etc. – who is involved in primary science in any way. To return to my first challenge, if we are to improve classroom practice, then much of the burden will fall on the subject leaders (co-ordinators as they are known) in science. It is they who will need to provide the lead, the drive and much of the enthusiasm to keep up the momentum in the teaching and learning that goes on in science in their schools. The work in schools, in turn, must be supported through a variety of networks. The ASE has an increasingly important role to play in providing the support for primary teachers, whether they are subject leaders or not. I am sure you will agree that the work of the ASE has been, and for the foreseeable future will continue to be, an integral part of the development of primary science.

And finally ...

Finally, I would like to think that, whatever happens to primary science in the future, it will always retain the vitality it has shown throughout its history to date. The sense of awe and wonder that scientific phenomena can elicit and the degree of curiosity that young children bring to their studies are two ingredients that must never be lost. Primary science has, for the most part, succeeded in capturing them up to now, so long may it continue.

Education

the space in which a child can grow?
the hole through which a child must go?

the height to which a mind can reach?
the syllabus to learn and teach?

the courage of a difficult truth?
the accelerated flight from youth?

the beauty of discordant song?
the rigidities of right and wrong?

the feel of sand, the burst of paint?
the pointed look and curt complaint?

the poppy in a field of wheat?
the curving back of a plastic seat?

the child at home and full of life?
the lonely child, the battered wife?

the breaker of moulds, free and wild?
the peachy cheeks of a sleeping child?

the wonder, the awe, the beauty, the best?
the feeling safe amongst the rest?

the space in which a child can grow?
the hole through which a child must go?

Neville Evans

What happened when?

1900

Queen Victoria dies
King Edward VII

Association of Public School Science Masters (later Science Masters' Association) formed (1901)

Elementary 'Board' schools

Nature Study Union

1910

First World War (1914–1918)
Major 'flu epidemic
Russian Revolution
Edward VII dies
King George V
Some women get the vote
Conscription introduced

Association of Science Teachers (later Association of Women Science Teachers) formed (1912)

Scholarships available for poorer children to attend Grammar schools

1920

General strike

Wall Street Crash

The Depression

English Elementary schools become Primary

Progressive Movement in education: importance of childhood/'nature'

Hadow Report (1)

1930

Spanish Civil War

George V dies
Edward VIII abdicates
King George VI

School leaving age = 14 years

Science = 'nature study'

40% UK income spent on welfare, inc. education

'School Certificate' on leaving

1940

Second World War (1939–1945)
Atomic bomb dropped on Hiroshima
National Health Service (NHS)
Independence for India and Pakistan

1944 Education Act

11+ exam. to Grammar school or Secondary Modern

Only 20% women enter Higher Education

1950

King George VI dies
Queen Elizabeth II
Clean Air Act
Major immigration from West Indies; later from Ireland

School leaving age = 15 years
O-level (Ordinary) and
A-level (Advanced) GCE introduced

1960

Berlin Wall built
Conscription ends

ASE formed from amalgamation of SMA and AWST (1963)

1st woman Prime Minister (Sri Lanka)
President Kennedy assassinated

1st man on the Moon

Miners' strike

Falklands War

Poll Tax revolt

Berlin Wall comes down

Tiananmen Square massacre, Beijing
Mandela released, President of S.A.
Death of Princess Diana
War in Kosova/Balkans

1st ASE Primary Science Sub-Committee (1963)

More employees in education than in military or civil defence

'Comprehensive' schools

School leaving age = 16 years

Nuffield Junior Science Project

Plowden Report

1970

End of free school milk

World number of universities doubled since 1950

Science 5/13

Learning Through Science project

Warnock Report

Full Committee status for ASE Primary Committee (1979)

1980

ASE Primary Science newsletter starts

Computers in schools

APU Report: Science at age 11

Nearly 40% women in UK in HE (50% in US, GDR)

SPACE Project

ESG Advisory Teachers for Science

National Curriculum for Science (1)

Primary Science Review (PSR) starts

1990

NC for science (2)

'Desirable Outcomes' for Early Years

NC for science (3)

More provision for Nursery staff and Teachers' Assistants

2000

NC for science (4)

Early Learning Goals

2001

Happy Birthday ASE!

131